Teaching
Synthetic
Phonics
IN PRIMARY SCHOOLS

SAGE was founded in 1965 by Sara Miller McCune to support the dissemination of usable knowledge by publishing innovative and high-quality research and teaching content. Today, we publish more than 750 journals, including those of more than 300 learned societies, more than 800 new books per year, and a growing range of library products including archives, data, case studies, reports, conference highlights, and video. SAGE remains majority-owned by our founder, and after Sara's lifetime will become owned by a charitable trust that secures our continued independence.

Los Angeles | London | Washington DC | New Delhi | Singapore

2ND EDITION

Teaching Synthetic Phonics

IN PRIMARY SCHOOLS

RHONA JOHNSTON & JOYCE WATSON

 |

Los Angeles | London | New Delhi
Singapore | Washington DC

Learning Matters
An imprint of SAGE Publications Ltd
1 Oliver's Yard
55 City Road
London EC1Y 1SP

SAGE Publications Inc.
2455 Teller Road
Thousand Oaks, California 91320

SAGE Publications India Pvt Ltd
B 1/I 1 Mohan Cooperative Industrial Area
Mathura Road
New Delhi 110 044

SAGE Publications Asia-Pacific Pte Ltd
3 Church Street
#10–04 Samsung Hub
Singapore 049483

Editor: Amy Thornton
Development editor: Jennifer Clark
Production controller: Chris Marke
Project management: Deer Park Productions
Marketing manager: Lorna Patkai
Cover design: Wendy Scott
Typeset by: C&M Digitals (P) Ltd, Chennai, India
Printed by Henry Ling Limited at The Dorset
Press, Dorchester DT1 1HD

First published in 2007 by Learning Matters Ltd
Second edition published 2014

Library of Congress Control Number: 2014949771

British Library Cataloguing in Publication Data

A catalogue record for this book is available
from the British Library

MIX
Paper from
responsible sources
FSC   FSC™ C013985
www.fsc.org

ISBN 978-1-4462-9861-9

At SAGE we take sustainability seriously. Most of our products are printed in the UK using FSC papers and boards. When
we print overseas we ensure sustainable papers are used as measured by the Egmont grading system.
We undertake an annual audit to monitor our sustainability.

Contents

About the authors

Rhona Johnston

After gaining her BA and PhD in Psychology, Rhona trained as a primary school teacher and was a learning support teacher for two years. She then joined the School of Psychology at the University of St Andrews, which she left after 20 years to take up a Readership in the School of Psychology at the University of Birmingham. For the past 13 years she has been a Professor in the Department of Psychology at the University of Hull. Rhona has researched extensively in the areas of reading disorders and reading development. She has served on six Department for Education committees overseeing the introduction of synthetic phonics teaching into schools in England, including contributing to the writing of a teaching programme and reviewing the guidelines for the construction of the Phonics Check. In 2012 she was awarded an MBE for services to Education.

Joyce Watson

Joyce was an Early Years teacher for a number of years, and then for over 20 years was a lecturer in the Northern College of Education in Dundee. Joyce holds an MEd from the University of Dundee, her thesis being in the field of reading comprehension. She also holds an Open University Diploma in Reading Development, and a PhD in Psychology from the University of St Andrews. Joyce's thesis was an investigation of the effects of phonics teaching on children's progress in reading and spelling.

Introduction

In 2005 the House of Commons Education and Skills Committee took written and oral evidence from us about our research on the initial teaching of reading. In its report the committee recommended an immediate review of the National Literacy Strategy (NLS) programme in view of our experimental evidence on the effectiveness of the synthetic phonics approach to teaching reading (paragraph 52, p23). In our study in Clackmannanshire in Scotland we had shown that synthetic phonics teaching led to better reading and spelling than the analytic phonics approach, the latter method closely resembling the NLS approach. We had found that children who had been taught by the synthetic phonics method not only read and spelt very much above average for their age, but that these gains increased year after year (Johnston and Watson, 2004, 2005a, 2005b). We later showed that at the age of 10 these children read and spelt better than children taught by the NLS programme *Progression in Phonics* (Johnston, McGeown and Watson, 2012). Following on from the Education and Skills Committee recommendations, the Rose Review (Rose, 2006) was set up to report on the best way to teach young children to learn to read. It concluded that the systematic synthetic phonics approach was the most effective. The recommendations of the Rose Review led to the publication of *Letters and Sounds* (DfES, 2007), which follows synthetic phonics principles and differs quite markedly from the previous NLS programme *Progression in Phonics*. In *Letters and Sounds* (DfES, 2007) children learn to sound and blend for reading very early on, and spend an equal amount of time on this activity as on segmenting spoken words for spelling. Furthermore, children are not taught to read words by sight, their sight word reading develops via the phonics pathway. *Progression in Phonics* (DfEE, 1999) uses an analytic phonics approach, introducing blending for reading later on, often at the end of the first year at school, or even at the start of the second year at school, and typically involves teaching children to read high frequency and common exception (tricky) words by sight. The supplementary programme *Playing with Sounds* (DfES, 2004) has an earlier introduction of blending for reading, but this is a minor activity compared with segmenting for spelling.

The purpose of this book is a) to give teachers and trainee teachers the necessary subject knowledge in order to understand the principles behind synthetic phonics, and b) to give practical guidance on how to carry out synthetic phonics lessons. Our book also explains c) how to carry out formative and summative assessment, so that slow learners receive appropriate support early on so that they can keep up with their classmates.

In Chapter 1, we introduce you to the debate about using whole language versus phonics teaching methods, and to the different types of phonic approaches. The terms analytic and synthetic phonics have been much misunderstood, and we have explained what these terms mean in the context of phonics teaching in the UK. We also outline our main findings on the relative effectiveness of these two types of phonics programmes. In Chapter 2 we discuss phonemes – what they are, how children develop awareness of them, and the role they play in learning to read. In Chapter 3 we describe the Simple View of Reading model used to underpin *Letters and Sounds* (DfES, 2007), which has replaced the searchlights model that was adopted for *Progression in Phonics* (DfEE, 1999). We also outline Ehri's (2005) model of reading development, which shows you the stages through which children progress to become skilled readers. Chapter 4 describes the new National Curriculum (DfE, 2013) and the implications it has for teaching; it is a statutory requirement that 'pupils should be taught to apply phonic knowledge as the route to decode words' (p19), including high frequency and common exception (tricky) words. We also explain the principles behind *Letters and Sounds* (DfES, 2007), in which children learn to read and spell single words by a synthetic phonics approach, but also learn to read captions and sentences from very early on. We also summarise Phases 1 to 6 of *Letters and Sounds* (DfES, 2007), of which Phases 2 to 6 involve phonics teaching.

Chapter 5 introduces you to the elements of a synthetic phonics programme, describing how to teach children to blend for reading and to segment for spelling. Chapter 6 shows you how to teach a complete synthetic phonics lesson in Phase 2, while Chapter 7 shows you how the same structure can be used to teach a lesson in Phase 5. In these two chapters we have also suggested how to organise the letter sequence recommended in *Letters and Sounds* (DfES, 2007) into weekly lesson plans. Throughout Chapters 5, 6 and 7 we also give guidance on how you can assess the progress your pupils are making, in order to give support early on to those who are progressing more slowly than their classmates. Chapter 8 describes the Phonics Screening Check used in England at the end of the second year at school (Year 1) from 2012, and how it has led to an improvement in the proportion of children reaching the expected level. We also explain how to assess children's phonics skills for formative assessment purposes, and include two diagnostic Phonics Checks that can be used for both formative and summative assessment. This chapter also describes the progress of a child with special needs who started school with severe language problems; he made excellent progress once he started a synthetic phonics programme and had a learning programme tailored to his needs. In Chapter 9 we outline the features of a systematic phonics teaching programme, give an overview of *Letters and Sounds*, and describe two popular commercial programmes, *Phonics Bug* (Watson and Johnston, 2010) and *Read Write Inc* (Miskin, 2011).

In conclusion, we hope that this book will help you understand how to implement a synthetic phonics approach to teaching reading and spelling in your classroom. It may seem complex at first, but you will find that it is very simple as the same lesson format can be used from Reception (Primary 1) right through to the end of Year 2 (Primary 3).

REFERENCES REFERENCES **REFERENCES** REFERENCES **REFERENCES** REFERENCES

DfE (2013) *The National Curriculum in England*. London: DfE. https://www.gov.uk/government/publications/national-curriculum-in-england-primary-curriculum (retrieved 20 May 2014).

DfEE (1999) *Progression in Phonics*. London: DfEE. No longer on government website. Available at http://www.amazon.co.uk/National-Literacy-Strategy-Progression-Whole-Class/dp/0193122375/ref=sr_1_1?s=books&ie=UTF8&qid=1394185289&sr=1-1&keywords=progression+in+phonics

DfES (2004) *Playing with Sounds: A Supplement to Progression Phonics*. London: DfES. No longer on government website. Available at http://www.amazon.co.uk/Playing-With-Sounds-Supplement-Progression/dp/B001PDS7U6

DfES (2007) *Letters and Sounds*. London: DfES. https://www.gov.uk/government/publications/letters-and-sounds (retrieved 27 August 2014).

Ehri, L.C. (2005) Development of Sight Word Reading: Phases and Findings. In Snowling, M.J. and Hulme, C. (Eds) *The Science of Reading: A handbook*. Oxford: Blackwell. pp135–54.

House of Commons Education and Skills Committee (2005) *Teaching children to read*. Eighth Report of Session 2004–05. London: The Stationery Office, Ltd. http://www.publications.parliament.uk/pa/cm200405/cmselect/cmeduski/121/121.pdf (retrieved 27 August 2014).

Johnston, R.S., McGeown, S. and Watson, J. (2012) Long-term effects of synthetic versus analytic phonics teaching on the reading and spelling ability of 10 year old boys and girls. *Reading and Writing*, 25, part 6, 1365–84. DOI: 10.1007/s11145-011-9323-x

Johnston, R.S and Watson, J. (2004) Accelerating the development of reading, spelling and phonemic awareness. *Reading and Writing*, 17(4), 327–57.

Johnston, R.S. and Watson, J. (2005a) A Seven Year Study of the Effects of Synthetic Phonics Teaching on Reading and Spelling Attainment. *Insight 17*. Edinburgh: Scottish Executive Education Department. SSN 1478-6796. Also available at http://www.scotland.gov.uk/Publications/2005/02/20682/52383 (retrieved 27 August 2014).

Johnston, R.S. and Watson, J. (2005b) The effects of synthetic phonics teaching on reading and spelling attainment, a seven year longitudinal study. Scottish Executive Education Department. http://www.scotland.gov.uk/Publications/2005/02/20688/52449 (retrieved 27 August 2014).

Miskin, R. (2011) *Read Write Inc Phonics Handbook*. Oxford: Oxford University Press.

Rose, J. (2006) *Independent Review of the Early Teaching of Reading*. Nottingham: DfES. http://webarchive.nationalarchives.gov.uk/20100408085953/http://standards.dcsf.gov.uk/phonics/rosereview/ (retrieved 27 August 2014).

Watson, J.E. and Johnston, R.S. (2010) *Phonics Bug*. Harlow: Pearson.

1
What is phonics and which type is the most effective?

Learning objectives

In this chapter, you will learn that:

- whole language approaches to teaching reading were common in the latter part of the twentieth century;
- in the 1990s there was concern in England that reading standards were falling because of this approach;
- unlike the whole language approach, phonic approaches draw children's attention to the fact letter sounds provide a good guide to the pronunciation of written words;
- with analytic phonics children initially learn some words by sight. This is followed by learning letter sounds in the initial, end and finally middle of words, and then learning to sound and blend;
- with synthetic phonics, children learn a few letter sounds and then learn to sound and blend right away;
- research shows that children learn to read and spell much better with synthetic phonics.

TEACHERS' STANDARDS

3. Demonstrate good subject and curriculum knowledge

Phonic approaches to teaching reading capitalise on the fact that our spelling system is alphabetic; that is, the letter sounds in words are a helpful, if sometimes imperfect, guide to pronunciation (see the Glossary for technical terms).

The earliest writing systems were not alphabetic, and indeed an alphabetic system is not well suited to all spoken languages. Very early writing systems used pictures, but obviously such systems are not good at coping with complex ideas as they are limited to picturable objects. Chinese uses a logographic writing system where one character represents a word, and where a sequence of characters forms a sentence. Alphabetic writing systems do the same thing, but here the individual sounds (or phonemes) of the spoken word are represented by letters, and a group of letters forms a word. Early sound-based writing systems, however, used representations at the syllable level, and in Phoenician script syllables were represented by their first consonants. The Greek alphabet was a major development as it introduced letters for each consonant and vowel, which stood for the phonemes in the spoken language. This is what we have in English. Once you have mastered an alphabet like ours, you can read unfamiliar words without having seen them before.

Phonics versus whole language approaches

There has long been a debate about whether children need to be taught that the English spelling system is alphabetic. Early approaches to teaching reading traditionally involved learning letter names or letter sounds (the latter being a major element of the phonics approach). However, a view developed that the phonics approach undermines children's ability to understand what they are reading (Adams, 1990, Chapter 2). The whole language approach to reading developed because of these concerns and also because of a change towards a child-centred educational philosophy. This development was very much influenced by the work of Piaget, who proposed that children were active learners, who constructed knowledge for themselves. These ideas were then applied to reading, although Piaget did not specifically address learning to read in his research, which was largely about the development of logical thinking. According to the whole language view that developed, reading should be meaning based. An unfamiliar word was to be identified as a whole unit by inferring its meaning from context, or even through picture cues, rather than the 'bottom up' approach of applying phonic knowledge to letters and letter sequences to decode the words.

REFLECTIVE TASK

Task 1

Here are a few short sentences. See if you can work out what the missing words are from the context:

The mouse ran into the ------, and hid under a ------. The cat ------ around and ---- put --- paws under the ------. --- popped the mouse and ran into the ------.

See the end of the chapter for answers.

Whole language methods were in vogue in England for much of the latter part of the twentieth century. The approach moved from being a method whereby children used their language skills to predict what a known word would be from the sentence context, which might aid reading fluency, to an approach whereby this was a major element in developing their ability to read an unfamiliar word. Where the guessed word is incorrect, however, children get misleading information that will undermine their ability to learn to recognise printed words; for low ability children it may be hard to over-ride the incorrect associations. This approach is particularly problematical for children with poor language skills, who will have greater difficulty in predicting the missing words, and whose reading problems will therefore be further compounded. See Chapter 3 for more about the distinction between reading comprehension and decoding printed words.

What was the perceived problem with phonics? One problem for some educationalists was that it involved direct instruction in the study of sub-parts of words, rather than operating at the getting meaning-from-text level. In addition, the type of phonics used in the UK, which was largely of the analytic type (see below), was many years ago implemented by drilling children in reading lists of similarly spelt words, i.e. word families. These programmes also tended to use phonic readers, some of which used very stilted language. It was argued that the phonic method was therefore unlikely to enthuse children about reading. Another objection to the method was that as some words in the English language are irregularly spelt, the phonic approach cannot be effective and leads to inaccurate pronunciation. The word 'yacht' is an extreme example of an irregular word that is not straightforward to read by a phonic approach (irregular words are called common exception words in England's National Curriculum, DfE, 2013). However, by the 1980s it was found that the standard of children's reading in England was dropping alarmingly (Turner, 1990), and the lack of phonics tuition was widely considered to be an element in the poor attainment figures. It seemed very likely that some children were not able to work out the alphabetic nature of the English spelling system without explicit tuition, and so made poor progress in learning to read.

Most Scottish primary schools retained phonics teaching, however, although the pace slowed down and the meaning-based aspect of the reading curriculum received greater emphasis. In the early 1990s it seemed to us that there was a general lack of knowledge about how phonics was taught, and we decided to examine how it was done in Scottish schools. We began a study in 1992 where we observed the phonics programme from the first to the third year of school in 12 classes (Watson, 1998). The approach used was of the analytic phonics type.

What is analytic phonics?

In analytic phonics, which until recently was the predominant phonic method in the UK, letter sounds are taught after reading has already begun, children initially learning to read some words by sight. We found in Scottish schools (Watson, 1998) that there was generally a long period devoted to learning the sounds of the letters of the alphabet. This generally started soon after school entry and took until Easter of the first year at school. In this phase, typically children would be shown whole words sharing a common initial letter sound, e.g. 'milk', 'man', 'mother' (Harris and Smith, 1976), attention being drawn to the /m/ sound heard at the beginning of the words. The children therefore would have some idea of the usefulness of letters sounds, but only at the beginning of words. They would probably recognise the rest of the word on a holistic basis, as the words presented were often suggested by the children and could be of quite complex structure. For example, a teacher would say 'This is the letter /m/', giving the sound and writing the letter on the blackboard. She would then ask the children for words beginning with the sound /m/, and write these on the board. In one lesson we observed a little boy said 'mallard' (there was a stream nearby), and the word went up on the board. After a minute or two there was a whole list of words starting with the letter 'm', listed one under each other on the blackboard. The point of the exercise was to show a family of words all starting with the letter 'm', and there was no attempt to pick words that were easy to read phonically.

We found that when all of the letter sounds had been taught in this way, attention would then be drawn to letter sounds at the ends of words. Finally, children learnt about the vowels in the middle of consonant-vowel-consonant (CVC) words. Although it is often thought that in analytic phonics the sounding and blending of letters to read unfamiliar words is not done, our observations in classes showed that this was a feature of such programmes. Indeed, in the region in which we were doing the study the teachers had an outline of the progression that their phonics teaching should take, and this was the third step. So towards the end of the first year at school, children in the study were taught to focus on letter sounds all through the word, and in some classes they were actively taught to sound and blend CVC words, e.g. /c/ /a/ /t/ -> cat.

We were very interested in the fact that our tests showed that once children were alerted to the importance of letter sounds in all positions in words, independent reading skill really took off. However, we did find that some schools were not teaching children to sound and blend. We were told that this was because researchers were saying at the time that it was impossible to blend the sounds in a way that made them sound like a word. We do tend to give consonant letter-sounds a following vowel sound, however hard we try not to, so the sounds in a word like 'cat' can come out as /cuh/ /ah/ /tuh/. However, children do manage to make the leap from these sounds to the whole word, perhaps partly because, as they start to sound and blend, a set of known words which look and sound like the unfamiliar word are activated in their memories (Johnston, 1998). The effectiveness of the approach may lie in the fact that the blending procedure teaches children to track through the letters in the word systematically from left to right. As each letter is fixated in turn, the sounds are produced, and this leads to the sequence of letters and sounds for the printed word being closely tied together in memory. This close attention to the letters and their sounds in an ordered sequence in words would inhibit children from looking only at distinctive features, such as end letters or letters sticking above or below the line, which would lead to a primitive form of sight word recognition. The importance of forming a more mature form of sight word recognition well underpinned by sound (or phonological) information will be described in more detail in Chapter 3.

We found that after reading CVC words through sounding and blending, children in analytic phonics programmes spent the next two years learning about consonant digraphs, consonant blends and vowel digraphs. (The term digraph refers to the spelling of one sound with two letters.) The children would typically be shown word families of similarly spelt words, that is, words with consonant digraphs, e.g. '<u>ch</u>in', '<u>ch</u>op', '<u>ch</u>ill'; initial consonant blends, '<u>st</u>ing', '<u>st</u>and', '<u>st</u>op'; final consonant blends, 'ma<u>st</u>', 'lo<u>st</u>', 'fi<u>st</u>'; vowel digraphs, 'c<u>oa</u>t', 'b<u>oa</u>t', 'fl<u>oa</u>t'; and split vowel digraphs, 'c<u>a</u>k<u>e</u>', 'b<u>a</u>k<u>e</u>', 'm<u>a</u>k<u>e</u>'. Consonant blends (described as adjacent consonants in *Letters and Sounds*, DfES, 2007) would be taught in the second year at school, as would some vowel digraphs, but the really difficult split vowel digraphs such as 'cake' would often be taught in the third year.

We were particularly interested in seeing how this phonic work was integrated with the rest of the reading programme, which had as its major aim that the children understood what they read; graded readers were generally introduced a month or so after starting school. Although phonic readers used to be widely available, by the early '90s we found schools were very often using non-phonic reading books in their programmes. We saw little integration of the phonic work and reading for meaning in the first year of school, as the children could not easily apply their phonic reading skills to the reading of books until they had learnt how to sound and blend all through words. At that point, of course, they could start to read unfamiliar words using this technique, but before that they had to recognise a word by sight, using a form of sight word recognition not well underpinned by letter-sound information.

Phonics in the National Curriculum

In order to improve the teaching of literacy in schools in England, the National Literacy Strategy was started in 1998. A Literacy Hour was established in which teachers were encouraged to teach phonics in addition to the whole language approach. *Progression in Phonics* (DfEE, 1999) was designed for use with children in Reception and Years 1 and 2, and it explained in detail how to implement a systematic phonics programme. As a first step, it was recommended that children be taught listening skills, e.g. to discriminate general environmental sounds, such as vehicle noises, birds singing, water being poured, etc. This progressed to the teaching of phonological awareness, that is, training children to hear rhymes and phonemes in spoken words. The actual phonics programme closely resembled what we had seen being done in Scotland, children being taught letter sounds at the beginning of words, then at the end, and then ultimately all through the words. At this point, children were taught to sound and blend letters in order to read unfamiliar words. However, in our studies we found only the faster learning children in England were sounding and blending before the end of the first year at school; most of the children started this procedure at the start of their second year at school, which was much later than we had observed in Scotland. The only difference between the actual content of the programmes by this stage was that the children in England were also taught to segment spoken words for spelling. However, we observed no gains for reading and spelling with this additional component, which was often taught in a play-like manner, and seemed to be designed largely to facilitate the development of the awareness of phonemes in spoken words (see Chapters 2 and 4). After the children had learnt the sounds of the letters of the alphabet, and how to blend and segment CVC words, they then learnt to read and spell words with consonant digraphs, e.g. 'thin', initial consonant blends, e.g. 'swim', final consonant blends, e.g. 'tent'. Finally, vowel digraphs were taught, showing, for example, that the vowel sound in 'fine' could also be spelt as in 'high', 'tie', and 'cry'.

A supplementary programme, *Playing with Sounds* (DfES, 2004), was a significant move towards a synthetic phonics approach. It introduced sounding and blending much earlier on, as early as after eight letter sounds had been taught. However, this activity was secondary to segmenting spoken words for spelling via the use of Phoneme Frames. As the children segmented the spoken word phoneme by phoneme in this activity, the appropriate letter would be put in the Phoneme Frame for each sound, working from left to right. Once all the letters were in place, the children then sounded and blended them. This task was also used as the primary means for teaching children the letters and their sounds. However, the Phoneme Frame task is not a synthetic phonics technique (see below); it is primarily about segmenting for spelling. Sounding and blending after a word has been spelt is a useful spelling-check process to ensure that the letters in the word are in the right order, but in this context it is not enabling the children to read an unfamiliar word as they already know what it is. A clear example of synthesis for reading is the Sound Buttons activity, where the children find out what the word is through blending the letter sounds. However, this task was recommended for introduction into the teaching programme after the Phoneme Frames task, and throughout the programme there were many more references to doing the Phoneme Frame and related tasks, and far fewer to doing the Sound Buttons activity. To add to the confusion between the two tasks, it was suggested that the Sound Buttons task could be used to read the words built up on the Phoneme Frame. Such usage with a known word would mean that this was no longer a synthetic phonics activity.

Huxford (2006) argues that phonics teaching should start with segmenting for spelling as young children are better at this than blending, so starting with segmenting fits the developmental progression. However, although blending is a difficult task, we have found that teaching it early on in the context of printed words is very effective. When it has a secondary role in a programme, the children's chance of acquiring the technique will be considerably reduced. Some children are slow to learn how to blend, but they have a better chance of understanding the procedure if it is repeatedly carried out in the classroom. While doing this they are also receiving a great deal of exposure to the printed word and its pronunciation, and to the importance of using letter sound cues to read unfamiliar words.

There are some other problems with classifying *Playing with Sounds* as a systematic synthetic phonics programme. It should have strongly advised teachers not to tell children to guess unfamiliar words from context or picture cues; this is a whole language approach that undermines the phonic method. The name of the programme gives a clue to another problem – it is primarily play orientated, as was *Progression in Phonics*. In our classroom observations of the latter, the play approach meant that many of the children did not seem to focus on the learning goals of the activity. It would be of interest to know just how effective *Playing with Sounds* was in developing reading and spelling skills, but the DfES did not carry out any testing of the programme's efficacy before launching it. This could have been done by testing children on standardised reading and spelling tests before and after the programme was carried out, and by comparing attainment with a control group using, for example, *Progression in Phonics*. We have not been able to study the effectiveness of *Playing with Sounds* as we have not found any schools to be implementing it; it was billed as a supplement to *Progression in Phonics* so it is possible that it was not thought by teachers to differ greatly from the previous programme.

Synthetic phonics

If analytic phonics in the UK often includes sounding and blending for reading, this raises the question of just what is so different about synthetic phonics. It is, as its name suggests, primarily about synthesising letter sounds in order to pronounce unfamiliar words. The critical difference is that with a synthetic phonics approach, shortly after starting school children learn just a few letter sounds and then start to sound and blend right away. Furthermore, new letter sounds are learnt very rapidly; as each new letter sound is learnt the children sound and blend the new words that can be formed with the taught letters. Words are not taught by sight, the children find out for themselves how to pronounce an unfamiliar word; it is very much an active learning method. Analytic phonics has a late onset of sounding and blending, or in some cases does not have it at all, and there is a lot of sight word learning. Letter sounds are learnt much more slowly and there is a long period in which children are taught letter sounds only at the beginning of words. We can think of phonics teaching as a continuum, with analytic phonics without blending at one end of the continuum and synthetic phonics at the other. The type of analytic phonics done in the UK sits somewhere in the middle, and might be described as analytic-then-synthetic phonics. This is where we would place the *Progression in Phonics* programme, as it had a late onset of sounding and blending. *Playing with Sounds* would be placed closer to synthetic phonics, but it had early sounding and blending as a minor activity, in the context of the major activity being segmenting the spoken word for spelling.

In our longitudinal study of analytic phonics in Scotland, we saw that children got a big boost in their independent reading skill when they started to sound and blend towards the end of the first year at school. We then started reading about synthetic phonics, looking particularly at Feitelson's (1988) description of how this is taught in Austria. It has often been said that such an approach for teaching reading works well in German, where there is a very regular spelling system, but that it cannot work in English as we have irregular words such as 'yacht'. If a child tries to sound this out, there might be a 'ch' sound in it, like in 'cheese'. However, 80–90% of words in English do have regular spellings (Adams, 1990). We decided that rather than concluding that an alphabetic approach such as synthetic phonics cannot be effective because of the existence of irregular words in English (Dombey, 2006), that the approach should be tested in actual practice.

We now need to look at synthetic phonics in a little more detail (we will describe how to implement it in Chapters 5, 6 and 7). It is a very accelerated form of phonics that does not begin by establishing an initial sight vocabulary. With this method, children are taught some letter sounds and how to sound and blend before they are introduced to books; however, books can be introduced early on (after six weeks of starting school in one of our studies). After the first few letter sounds have been taught, children are shown how these sounds can be blended together to find out the pronunciation of unfamiliar words (Feitelson, 1988). For example, when taught the letter sounds /s/ /a/ /t/ and /p/ the children can blend the letters in the words 'at', 'sat', 'tap', 'pat', 'pats', 'taps', 'a tap' etc., to find out what the word is. The children are not told the pronunciation of the new word by the teacher. Thus children can construct the pronunciation for themselves, so this is a self-teaching approach. Most of the letter–sound correspondences, including some vowel digraphs, can be taught in the space of a few months at the start of the first year at school, and consonant blends, such as 'clap', do not need to be taught at all. This means that from very early on children can read many of the unfamiliar words that they meet in text for themselves, without the assistance of the teacher. Although not traditionally part of synthetic phonics, in our studies we did also teach children how to segment spoken words for spelling. There was an equal split between the two activities, and sounding and blending for reading always came before segmenting for spelling in the lessons. In our studies, children were also taught irregular words from early on, so that they soon learnt that some words have a less than straightforward relationship between letters and sounds. However, they were not taught to recognise these words by sight, they had their attention drawn to the unusual part of the spelling, and also to the parts which could be sounded and blended.

Comparisons of the effectiveness of analytic and synthetic phonics teaching

In our studies we measured reading and spelling using standardised tests, where average performance for age is worked out by measuring the skills of representative samples of children. This means that we know how many items in the test a child needs to get right to be performing at the typical level for their age. For example, we used the British Ability Scales Word Reading Test (Elliott *et al.*, 1977) to assess children's ability to read isolated words. There are 90 words in the test, and by counting up the number of words correct you can work out a child's reading age; on this test children can score at a level appropriate for a five-year-old, right up to the level expected for a child aged 14 years and 5 months. We measured spelling using the Schonell spelling test (Schonell and Schonell, 1952), which tests children's ability to spell isolated words. We also measured reading comprehension using the Primary Reading Test (France, 1981) until the end of the third year at school, and from then on adopted the Group Reading Test (Macmillan Unit, 2000).

In our study in Clackmannanshire, we examined the effects of three types of phonics programmes on the reading and spelling of children in their first year of school (Primary 1 in Scotland, equivalent to Reception in England). The programmes lasted for 16 weeks, for 20 minutes a day. One group of children learnt by the synthetic phonics approach, another learnt by the analytic phonics approach (based on the pace and approach typically used in the schools), and a third group spent half their time doing analytic phonics and half their time learning to blend and segment phonemes in spoken words (phonological awareness training). All of the children, regardless of research condition, started reading books six weeks after the start of the programme.

Those children learning by the two analytic phonics programmes read and spelt about right for their age, but the ones learning by the synthetic phonics method were seven months ahead of what would be expected for their age in word reading and spelling (Johnston and Watson, 2004, Experiment 1).

It is often said that children who learn to read by a synthetic phonics approach will have difficulty with reading irregular (common exception) words. We examined this in our study, and found that at the end of the training period the synthetic-phonics taught children read irregular words, such as 'one' and 'said', better than those taught by the analytic phonics method (Johnston and Watson, 2004, Experiment 1). We also found that only the children taught by the synthetic phonics approach could read words by analogy at this stage, being able, for example, to work out the pronunciation of 'sing' from the known word 'ring' (Johnston and Watson, 2004, Experiment 1).

Synthetic phonics is a fast-moving approach, with letter sounds being taught very rapidly, and with an early start to sounding and blending, whereas analytic phonics in the UK is typically slow moving. It might be the case that if an analytic phonics programme was speeded up, so that letter sounds were learnt equally fast, the children's reading and spelling would be as good as those taught by synthetic phonics. However, we have found that this is not the case in another study; even after the analytic-phonics taught children learnt to sound and blend in class they still did not catch up (Johnston and Watson, 2004, Experiment 2). In this study the children continued with their analytic phonics classroom programmes throughout the study and carried out the synthetic phonics training, if done, on top of this. As synthetic phonics includes the teaching of letter sounds at the beginning of words it subsumes the analytic phonics approach, but additionally draws attention to the role of letter sounds in the middle and end of words right from the start, rather than towards the end of the first year at school, as is done in analytic phonics in the UK.

We cannot look at the long-term effects of analytic phonics teaching in the Clackmannanshire study because after our first post-test at Easter the children learnt to read by the synthetic phonics method for ethical reasons. However, we do have data from the study where we examined analytic phonics teaching for three years in Scottish schools. In Figure 1.1 we compare the long-term effects of analytic phonics teaching with the long-term effects of synthetic phonics teaching. Primary 1 is equivalent to Reception in England. The left-hand side of the figure shows the children's performance at the end of the first year at school (after both groups had learnt to sound and blend), and the right-hand side shows their performance at the end of the third year at school. To make the graphs easy to read we have subtracted the children's chronological ages from their reading and spelling ages. A positive score (where the top of a bar is above the zero line) means that the children have performed above what would be expected for their age. Where the bar is below zero, the children are performing below what is expected for their age. You can see that the analytic phonics children were behind the synthetic phonics group in word reading, spelling, and reading comprehension at the end of the first year at school, and were still behind at the end of the third year at school. In many cases, they were also performing below what was expected for their age level. This was despite the fact that the analytic phonics teaching had covered the same ground as the synthetic phonics teaching by the end of the third year at school.

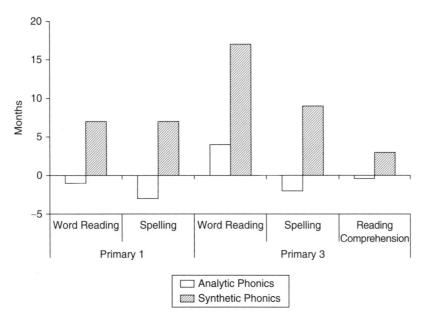

Figure 1.1 Gains in reading and spelling compared with age in Primary 1 and 3, analytic versus synthetic phonics

We also found in the Clackmannanshire Study that an early start to synthetic phonics led to better results than a later start. When tested at the end of the second year at school, the children who had done synthetic phonics from early on were better spellers than those who had done analytic phonics first (Johnston and Watson, 2004, Experiment 1). A similar pattern was found in word reading for girls, who did better if they had done synthetic phonics early (Johnston and Watson, 2005).

Effects of synthetic phonics teaching on the reading of boys and girls

When we looked at how boys performed compared to girls in our longitudinal study of analytic phonics teaching, we were not surprised to find at the end of the third year at school that they performed less well across the board in word reading, spelling and reading comprehension. Many studies throughout the world have shown that boys read less well than girls (e.g. Mullis *et al.*, 2003). The boys in our longitudinal analytic phonics study read words three months above what was expected for their chronological age, but were four months behind for their age in spelling, and five months behind in reading comprehension. The girls were reading words six months above chronological age and were age appropriate in spelling and reading comprehension. However, when we saw how the boys performed when learning by the synthetic phonics method at the end of the third year at school we were very surprised. Not only did they do as well as the girls in spelling and reading comprehension (nine months ahead of age in spelling, and three months ahead in comprehension) but they actually read words significantly better (see Figure 1.2). Thus, boys read words 20 months ahead of age, while the girls read around 14 months ahead (Johnston and Watson, 2005). Both boys and girls read words much better than was the average for their age with synthetic phonics teaching, but the gain was much larger for the boys.

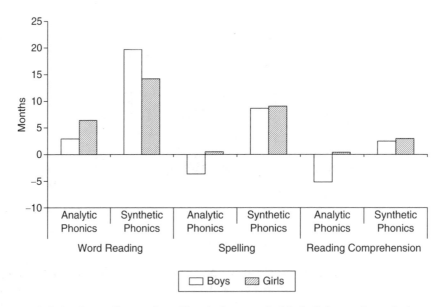

Figure 1.2 Gains in reading and spelling in boys and girls in Primary 3, analytic versus synthetic phonics

This advantage in word reading for boys was sustained right until the end of our study, being found even when the children were aged 11 and were in the seventh year of school. By that stage, the boys were also significantly better spellers. Figure 1.3 shows mean reading, spelling and chronological ages. We do not yet know why this approach is so effective for boys, but there is evidence that boys work best in a structured situation (Naglieri and Rojahn, 2001). Synthetic phonics is very structured, and indeed has a 'constructional' element in the way we implement it, even using plastic letters in the early stages (see Chapters 5, 6 and 7), which may particularly suit boys.

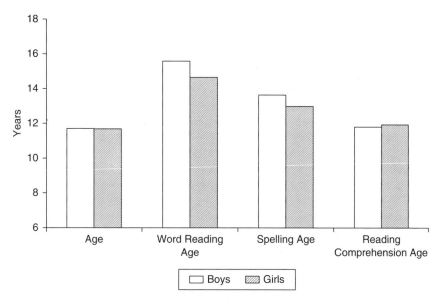

Figure 1.3 Reading and spelling in 11-year-old boys and girls taught by the synthetic phonics method

Effects of synthetic phonics on children from areas of deprivation

Research has shown that from the very first year at school, children from areas of deprivation perform less well in reading than those from more advantaged areas (Stuart *et al.*, 1998; Duncan and Seymour, 2000). We found that with synthetic-phonics teaching children from less well-off areas only started to fall behind the more advantaged children in word reading, spelling and reading comprehension towards the end of primary schooling (Johnston and Watson, 2005), but even then these comparisons were not statistically significant (see Figure 1.4). By the end of primary schooling, the children from areas of deprivation were reading words six months behind the level of the children from more advantaged areas. However, the children from areas of deprivation were still reading around 38 months ahead of what was expected for their age, and their spelling was 16 months ahead of age level (Johnston and Watson, 2005). Reading comprehension was age appropriate, which is noteworthy as reading comprehension depends on general language skills, and these skills are usually less well developed in children from areas of deprivation.

Over the whole sample, by this stage the children were reading words 42 months ahead of age, spelling was 20 months ahead, and reading comprehension was 3.5 months ahead. In all cases, performance was statistically ahead of what would be expected for chronological age, despite the sample having a verbal ability score of 93 (where the average is 100).

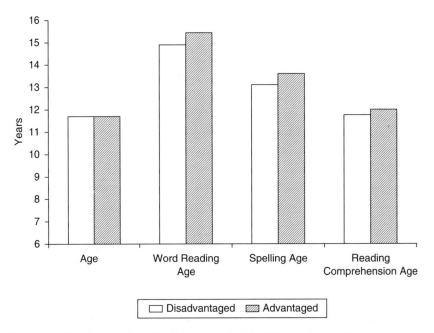

Figure 1.4 Reading and spelling in 11-year-old children from advantaged and disadvantaged backgrounds

There was also a low level of underachievement. For example, at the end of the second year at school, only 2% of children (regardless of social background) were reading words more than a year below what was expected for their age, and none was as much as two years behind. Even at the end of the seventh year at school, only 13 out of 236 children (5.6%) were reading words more than two years below their age level.

Why is this method of teaching so effective for children from areas of deprivation? Stuart *et al.* (1998) suggest that one major inequality for such children when starting school is their lack of letter knowledge; these children are less likely to have been carrying out literacy-related learning at home. However, with synthetic phonics this disadvantage is very quickly overcome because of the rapidity with which letters sounds are learnt, producing a level playing field for them.

Another view is that children from areas of deprivation in particular are handicapped by starting school with low levels of phoneme awareness, finding it very hard, for example, to segment a spoken word like 'cat' into phonemes, e.g. /c/ /a/ /t/. Harrison (2004) argues that children will find it impossible to gain much from phonics tuition without prior phonemic awareness ability. In our study in Clackmannanshire, we have examined the progress of the children who started school with no phoneme or rhyme awareness skills at all (Johnston and Watson, 2004, Experiment 1). After 16 weeks of synthetic phonics teaching, this group scored 45% correct on the phoneme awareness test, whereas the group learning by analytic phonics with an additional phonological-awareness training programme scored 22%. Even more importantly, at the end of the second year at school, when all the 'at risk' children had learnt by the synthetic phonics approach, these children were reading words around six months ahead of chronological age, and were spelling over eight months ahead of age. You can read more about phoneme awareness in Chapter 2, but we can conclude for the moment that synthetic phonics is very effective at developing phoneme awareness, and does not need to be preceded by a phoneme awareness training programme (carried out without the support of letters and print) in order to get excellent results.

Comparison of the long-term effectiveness of synthetic phonics teaching in Clackmannanshire with *Progression in Phonics* in England

We have published a study comparing the children in Clackmannanshire at the age of 10, who learnt by the synthetic phonics approach, with children of the same age in England who had learnt via *Progression in Phonics* (DfEE, 1999), an analytic phonics approach that includes a lot of sight word teaching (Johnston *et al.*, 2012). It was found that children taught by the synthetic phonics approach read words, spelt words and had reading comprehension skills significantly in advance of those taught by the analytic phonics method. For example, using age-standardised scores with a mean of 100, the synthetic phonics taught children got a mean word reading score of 108.2, and the *Progression in Phonics* sample got a mean score of 98.0. We were particularly interested in how boys performed compared to girls. We found that the boys taught by the synthetic phonics method had better word reading than the girls in their classes, and their spelling and reading comprehension was as good. On the other hand, the boys taught by the analytic phonics method, although they performed as well as the girls in word reading, had inferior spelling and reading comprehension. It seems likely that boys need better word recognition ability in order to have equivalent spelling and reading comprehension skills compared with girls, and we have shown that the synthetic phonics approach is particularly effective in developing that skill in boys.

In a meta-analysis of a large number of studies, Ehri *et al.* (2001) showed that the treatment advantage found for phonics versus non-phonics programmes declined over time. However, we found that our synthetic phonics sample showed an increase in their word reading scores compared with chronological age over time, and that the boys showed a steeper positive trajectory than the girls (Johnston *et al.* 2012). Similarly, J. Torgesen *et al.*'s (1999) study of children at risk of reading failure showed that the gains shown by the synthetic phonics taught children in word reading increased over time compared to those receiving embedded phonics tuition. It seems likely that this is because the synthetic phonics approach is a very effective self-teaching method.

We also examined in this study whether children taught by the synthetic phonics approach had any difficulties in reading irregular words compared with those taught by

Progression in Phonics, where the children were taught to read these words by sight without phonic analysis. Children learning by the synthetic phonics method had had their attention drawn to the unusual grapheme–phoneme correspondences in irregular words, but had also been shown the regular correspondences in these words, learning that all words have a decodable element. The synthetic phonics taught children showed no impairment in reading irregular words compared with the analytic phonics taught sample.

Meta-analysis on the effectiveness of synthetic phonics versus analytic phonics teaching

Despite all of these findings, Wyse and Styles (2007) have argued that there is 'no strong RCT (randomised controlled trial) evidence that any one form of systematic phonics is more effective than any other' (p37). This is untrue as such a study was published in 2004 (Johnston and Watson, 2004, Experiment 2), which the study in Clackmannanshire replicated. However, it is worth looking at the findings from meta-analyses. With this approach a review of many studies is carried out, data from all the relevant studies are extracted, and a statistical analysis is conducted covering all of the studies. It is not easy to combine studies in this way as teaching interventions may differ greatly in the training programmes used, and the length of the training involved. It is the role of the reviewers to categorise the studies into meaningful groupings and to decide which post-test data points it is appropriate to include. Such an analysis has been attempted by C. Torgerson *et al.* (2006), following on from the meta-analysis carried out by the National Reading Panel (NRP) (Ehri *et al.*, 2001).

The NRP meta-analysis compared the effects of systematic phonics instruction with the effects of unsystematic or no systematic phonics instruction. Ehri *et al.* (2001) reviewed the entire literature available from 1970, and found that only 37% of studies had a randomised controlled trial design. This design is hard to implement in educational research if teaching in the research conditions is done on a whole class basis; it is much easier when children can be randomly assigned to conditions. However, by analysing the randomised controlled trial studies separately and comparing them with the controlled trial literature, they found no significant differences in the pooled estimates of effect size. Thus, systematic phonics instruction was found to be more effective in developing children's reading skills than all other forms of control instruction, in both the controlled trial and the randomised controlled trial studies.

Despite the NRP's findings, the meta-analysis carried out by C. Torgerson *et al.* (2006) on the effectiveness of phonics teaching, which has not been published in a peer-reviewed journal, only used randomised controlled trial studies and ignored controlled trial studies. Unlike the NRP study, they also compared the effectiveness of synthetic phonics versus analytic phonics programmes; the NRP probably did not do this because of the paucity of the literature. Indeed, the NRP say:

effect sizes based on larger numbers of comparisons are more reliable and representative of the population than effect sizes based on small numbers. In interpreting effect sizes, particularly those that are not statistically significant, it is important to note whether the number of studies was sufficient to yield acceptable statistical power. (Ehri et al., 2001, p403)

C. Torgerson *et al.* (2006) found only two published randomised controlled trial studies comparing synthetic phonics and analytic phonics. The NRP only selected published studies, and concluded from their analyses that this did not lead to a systematic bias in outcome. However, C. Torgerson *et al.* (2006) included an unpublished study (Skailand, 1971) in their meta-analysis. Their rationale for this was that there is a well-established tendency for trials that produce negative effects to be less likely to be published than positive trials. However, the Skailand (1971) study reported a significant effect on one of the post-test measures, so the fact that it has never been published suggests doubt about its quality. Indeed, there is a serious problem with this study; half of the training for the kindergarten children was carried out using silent 'e' words, such as 'tape' and 'rode', as well as words like 'tap' and 'rod'. In the synthetic phonics programme *Letters and Sounds* (2007) silent 'e' words are taught much later on, in the second year at school, because children at the beginning stages of reading by a synthetic phonics approach would mis-read words like 'tape' as 'tapee'. We also need to note that C. Torgerson *et al.* (2006) put the wrong figures from this study into their meta-analysis, as they used performance on the words on which the children had been *trained* (where there was a significant treat-ment effect), although scores for performance on untrained items were also available (where there was no significant treatment effect). The NRP (Ehri *et al.*, 2001) scrupulously excluded using post-test scores taken from performance on the trained items; the aim of these meta-analyses is to determine what teaching methods will lead to an improvement in general reading ability, not just to gains on the items that have been taught.

Published studies of synthetic phonics

This leaves just two published randomised controlled trial studies on synthetic phonics that can be validly included in a meta-analysis. One study compared the effects of syn-thetic versus analytic phonics teaching (Johnston and Watson, 2004, Experiment 2). This was a study of new school entrants who carried out a 10-week intervention for half an hour a week in their first term at school. All of the groups were exposed to the same new print vocabulary in their training, and the speed of learning letter sounds was equated for the analytic and synthetic phonics groups. The second study was by J. Torgesen *et al.* (1999), comparing the effects of embedded phonics (EP) and phoneme awareness plus synthetic phonics (PASP) teaching on a highly selected sample of children at risk of reading failure. This was a five-term intervention, starting in the second semester of kindergarten, and terminating at the end of second grade. The phoneme awareness and synthetic phonics condition used a well-known programme that aims to lead children to discover and label the articulatory gestures associated with phonemes prior to learning to read (p582, column 1, lines 44–9). Ehri *et al.* (2001) describe how children using this method are taught, for example, that the spoken word 'beat' consists of a lip popper, a smile sound, and a tongue tapper. The children in J. Torgesen *et al.*'s (1999) study would have learnt to track sounds in spoken words with mouth pictures, coloured blocks, and finally letters; this means that they would not have been taught to read words right at the start of their training programme. This condition was contrasted with an embedded phonics (EP) programme, which, unlike the phoneme awareness plus synthetic phonics condition, started with early word recognition work (p582, column 2, lines 8–10). This programme is not exactly the same as analytic phonics in the UK, but does have some similarities, as there was instruction in letter–sound correspondences in the context of the sight words being learnt and even a little sounding and blending. To summarise, the embedded phonics programme had an early start to learning to recognise printed words, but this work began much later in the phoneme awareness plus synthetic phonics condition, as the philosophy behind this approach is that children at risk of reading failure need to develop phoneme awareness before learning to read.

Revisiting the C. Torgerson *et al.* (2006) meta-analysis

Using Johnston and Watson's (2004, Experiment 2) word recognition scores from the post-test carried out at the end of training, C. Torgerson *et al.* (2006) calculated an effect size of 1.32, favouring synthetic phonics. This is a very large effect, as an effect size of 0.2 is considered to be small, an effect size of 0.5 is seen as medium, and an effect size of 0.8 is seen as large. The J. Torgesen *et al.* (1999) intervention lasted for 2.5 years, and multiple post-tests were reported. In the NRP study, Ehri *et al.* (2001) explained that they calculated effect sizes at three test points: 1) at the end of instruction or at the end of one year if instruction lasted longer, 2) at the end of instruction, 3) at follow-up points after a delay ranging from four months to one year. Given the number of studies in the NRP meta-analysis, these varying test points made little difference to the pooled estimates of effect size they calculated. However, it makes a huge difference to the effect sizes calculated for the J. Torgesen *et al.* (1999) training study. The study started in the second semester of kindergarten, and continued for five semesters. At the end of the first semester (after about 18 hours of tuition, when the synthetic phonics group was doing phoneme awareness training rather than reading), C. Torgerson *et al.* (2006) calculated an effect size of -0.25 for the comparison between the word reading skills of the synthetic and embedded (analytic-type) phonics groups, showing a small effect favouring analytic phonics. It was this figure that they put into the meta-analysis. However, J. Torgesen *et al.* (1999) concluded that the *synthetic* phonics condition was the most effective one in their study. In order to understand the disagreement between C. Torgerson *et al.* (2006) and J. Torgesen *et al.* (1999) about what the study showed, it is instructive to examine the effect sizes at the end of the intervention, that is, at the end of Grade 2. For the full sample, looking at reading on the word recognition test, there is an effect size of 0.44, favouring synthetic phonics; this is why the authors concluded that the phoneme awareness plus synthetic phonics condition was the most effective in developing word reading skills. It is also noteworthy that in an analysis of the proportion of children who had been held back a grade, J. Torgesen *et al.* (1999) found that 25% of the embedded phonics group children had been retained, compared to only 9% of the phoneme awareness plus synthetic phonics group. When these children were removed from the analysis, this sub-sample yielded an effect size of 0.74, favouring synthetic phonics.

We have recalculated the pooled estimates of effect size calculated on J. Torgesen *et al.*'s (1999, full sample) and Johnston and Watson's (2004, Experiment 2) post-test data from the end of their interventions. Using the fixed effects model, the pooled estimate of the effect size was 0.77, p<.0001. Using the random effects model, the pooled estimate of effect size was 0.86, p<.05. These effect sizes are considered large. Furthermore, if these calculations are carried out using the data from J. Torgesen *et al.*'s (1999) sub-sample, the pooled estimate of effect size over the two studies is 1.04, p<.0001, fixed effects model, and 1.03, p<.0004, random effects model. In both cases, the pooled estimates of effect size strongly favour synthetic phonics.

In the controlled trial Clackmannanshire study (Johnston and Watson, 2004, Experiment 1), an effect size of 0.84 was found, which is also large. One of the concerns about controlled trial studies is that they may inflate effect sizes; this is clearly not the case here as the randomised controlled trial study (Johnston and Watson, 2004, Experiment 2) was found to lead to an effect of even greater magnitude (effect size 1.32). Furthermore, it should also be noted that elsewhere in their report, C. Torgerson *et al.* (2006) argued that Johnston and Watson's (2004, Experiment 1) finding that children learnt to read better with synthetic phonics was largely due to regression to the mean, a statistical artefact, as these children came from more deprived homes than the children in the analytic phonics condition. Regression to the mean is a phenomenon that affects *actual* scores, whereby very low scorers perform closer to the mean on a re-test, and very high scorers do the same. However, this cannot have operated in this study, as nearly all of the children, regardless of group, were non-readers on the standardised test of word reading administered at the start of the study, so there were no scores that could regress to the mean.

Conclusions on C. Torgerson *et al.*'s (2006) meta-analysis

There is a very small literature comparing the effects of synthetic versus analytic (or similar) phonics teaching. Meta-analyses ought not be attempted on only three studies; the technique is designed to enable conclusions to be drawn over a large literature, and analyses on a small literature may well be unreliable. This is all the more the case if errors are made in deciding which studies should be included, and which data should be entered into the calculations. In the C. Torgerson *et al.* (2006) analysis, the authors included an unpublished study with an invalid implementation of the synthetic phonics method, and they also used the wrong post-test data. Another problem is that they selected post-test data from very early on in the J. Torgesen *et al.* (1999) study, at a stage when one group was doing a method that develops early sight word reading (embedded phonics condition) and the other group was largely developing phoneme awareness skills in the absence of print (phoneme awareness plus synthetic phonics condition).

The conclusion by C. Torgerson *et al.* (2006) that there is no strong randomised controlled trial evidence that any one form of systematic phonics is more effective than any other is not justified. Two published randomised controlled trial studies have found synthetic phonics to be much more effective than analytic-type phonics, for both normal school entrants and those at risk of reading failure. These findings have been replicated in the larger controlled trial study carried out in Clackmannanshire, which was implemented by teachers on a whole class basis (Johnston and Watson, 2004, Experiment 1), where new school entrants, a high proportion of whom were at risk of reading failure, made very much better progress with synthetic than analytic phonics. These gains for synthetic phonics have been shown to be long term and to increase in strength year after year; the approach has also been shown to lead to better word reading, spelling and reading comprehension than the English *Progression in Phonics* programme (Johnston and Watson, 2005; Johnston *et al.*, 2012).

Reactions to the synthetic phonics studies

The C. Torgerson *et al.* (2006) meta-analysis focussed on our randomised controlled trial study (Johnston and Watson, 2004, Experiment 2), which the study in Clackmannanshire replicated. It has been claimed, however, that the gains the children in Clackmannanshire made with this method were not due to the synthetic phonics teaching at all but were due to other interventions being carried out concurrently (Ellis, 2005, 2007, p288). On the basis of conversations that Ellis had with teachers in Clackmannanshire, she has claimed that the gains were due to the introduction of nursery nurses into Primary 1, story bags, home–school link teachers, homework clubs and nurture groups. In fact the only activities co-occurring with our study were a 'books for babies' scheme, and the appointment of four home–school link workers. However, the home–school link workers were not allowed to support parents with literacy or to help in the class-room during the research intervention. Furthermore, although two of these home–school link workers were placed in schools in the synthetic phonics condition, there were also two in schools in the analytic phonics plus phoneme awareness condition. Given that the children in the latter condition performed significantly less well than the children in the synthetic phonics condition, the presence of home–link workers cannot account for the superior performance of the children in the synthetic phonics condition.

Ellis (2007) uses information from the Scottish 5–14 national testing for the study schools in Primary 7 to argue that the children in the study schools were not perform-ing above age expectations. However, 22% of the pupils in these schools were not in our intervention, so these overall figures for classes are not comparable with our own data. Furthermore, these national tests are unstandardised and are administered by class teachers at any time in the year when they feel that a child or group of children have attained a 5–14 level. Indeed, Ellis (2007) concedes that such testing should not be seen as a direct challenge to the standardised tests we used. That is certainly the case, as the figures she presented showed that some of the schools in the disadvan-taged areas outperformed those in the advantaged areas on the national tests. This is a surprising outcome in itself, but particularly so as we found that the children from better-off areas had started to pull ahead of the children from less advantaged homes at this point. The standardised reading comprehension test we used, on the other hand, has been shown to be a good predictor of the English national test scores for reading (Macmillan Unit, 2000).

Leaving aside comparisons of reading performance with age expectations, it is useful to look at how well the children in the study in Clackmannanshire performed in read-ing compared with children in England taught by *Progression in Phonics* (DfEE, 1999). We found that at the age of 10 the children in Clackmannanshire had significantly better word reading, spelling and reading comprehension (Johnston *et al.*, 2012). They also did not differ in how positive they were about reading (Johnston *et al.*, 2009). It should also be noted that since introducing synthetic phonics teaching in England, there has been an increase in the percentage of children reaching the required level in the Key Stage 1 national reading assessments, which measure reading comprehension. It was found in 2012 that 2% more children reached the expected level in reading in 2012 than the previous year (estimated to be around 7,500 children, taking into account differences in the sizes of the cohorts), and in 2013 this went up a further 2% (DfE, 2013). In terms of decoding ability, in 2012 58% of children in Year 1 passed the new Phonics Check, and in 2013 69% passed. Therefore there is evidence that the introduction of the synthetic phonics teaching method has led to improvements in both word reading and reading comprehension in England.

A SUMMARY OF **KEY POINTS**

➢ English has an alphabetic writing system, and only a small percentage of words are irregular, e.g. 'yacht'.

➢ Some children do not notice the alphabetic nature of our spelling system without direct tuition.

➢ A synthetic phonics approach teaches letter sounds very rapidly; an analytic phonics approach teaches them much more slowly.

➢ A synthetic phonics approach introduces sounding and blending early on; an analytic phonics approach introduces it much later on or not at all.

➢ Children's reading really takes off when they learn to sound and blend to pronounce unfamiliar words.

➢ Children learning by the analytic phonics approach did not catch up in reading with those taught by a synthetic phonics approach, even after sounding and blending was introduced.

➢ Boys read and spell better than girls with synthetic phonics (but girls do very well).

➢ Children from areas of deprivation keep up with more advantaged children in reading and spelling until near the end of primary schooling, and even then are performing well above what would be expected for their age.

➢ Synthetic phonics develops phoneme awareness skills better than direct teaching of these skills.

➢ There are long-term gains with synthetic phonics teaching, and the gains over chronological age have been found to increase year after year.

REFLECTIVE TASK

Task 1 answers

The mouse ran into the <u>garden</u>, and hid under a <u>bucket</u>. The cat <u>prowled</u> around and <u>then</u> put <u>her</u> paws under the <u>bucket</u>. <u>Out</u> popped the mouse and ran into the <u>bushes</u>.

REFERENCES REFERENCES **REFERENCES** REFERENCES REFERENCES REFERENCES

Adams, M.J. (1990) *Beginning to read: Learning and thinking about print*. London: MIT.

DfE (2013) *The National Curriculum in England*. London: DfE. https://www.gov.uk/government/publications/national-curriculum-in-england-framework-for-key-stages-1-to-4 (retrieved 17 March 2014).

DfE (2013) *Phonics Screening Check and National Curriculum Assessments at Key Stage 1 In England, 2012/13*. London: DfE. https://www.gov.uk/government/uploads/system/uploads/attachment_data/file/245813/SFR37-2013_Text.pdf (retrieved 27 August 2014).

DfEE (1999) *Progression in Phonics*. London: DfEE. No longer on government website. Available at http://www.amazon.co.uk/National-Literacy-Strategy-Progression-Whole-Class/dp/0193122375/ref=sr_1_1?s=booksandie=UTF8andqid=1394185289andsr=1-1and-keywords=progression+in+phonics

DfES (2004) *Playing with Sounds: A Supplement to Progression Phonics*. London: DfES. No longer on government website. Available at http://www.amazon.co.uk/Playing-With-Sounds-Supplement-Progression/dp/B001PDS7U6

DfES (2007) *Letters and Sounds*. London: DfES. https://www.gov.uk/government/publications/letters-and-sounds (retrieved 27 August 2014).

Dombey, H. (2006) Phonics and English Orthography. In M. Lewis and S. Ellis (Eds) *Phonics. Practice, Research, Policy*. London: Paul Chapman Publishing. pp95–104.

Duncan, L.G. and Seymour, P.H.K. (2000) Socio-economic differences in foundation level literacy. *British Journal of Psychology*, 91, 145–66.

Ehri, L., Nunes, S., Stahl, S. and Willows, D. (2001) Systematic phonics instruction helps students learn to read: Evidence from the National Reading Panel's meta-analysis. *Review of Educational Research*, 71, 393–447.

Elliott, C.D., Murray, D.J. and Pearson, L.S. (1977) *The British Ability Scales*. Windsor: NFER Nelson.

Ellis, S. (2005) Phonics is just the icing on the cake. *TES Scotland*. 23 September.

Ellis, S. (2007) Policy and research: Lessons from the Clackmannanshire Synthetic Phonics Initiative. *Journal of Early Childhood Literacy*, 7, 281–97.

Feitelson, D. (1988) Facts and Fads in Beginning Reading. *A Cross-Language Perspective*. Norwood, NJ: Ablex.

France, N. (1981) *Primary Reading Test*. Windsor: NFER-Nelson.

Harris, L.A. and Smith, C.B. (1976) *Reading Instruction: Diagnostic Teaching in the Classroom* (2nd Edition). London: Holt, Rinehart and Winston.

Harrison, C. (2004) *Understanding reading development*. London: Sage.

Huxford, L. (2006) Phonics in Context: Spelling Links. In M. Lewis and S. Ellis (Eds) *Phonics. Practice, Research, Policy*. London: Paul Chapman Publishing. pp83–103.

Johnston, R.S. (1998) The case for orthographic knowledge – A reply to Robert Scholes. *Journal of Research in Reading*, 21, 195–200.

Johnston, R.S., McGeown, S. and Watson, J. (2012) Long-term effects of synthetic versus analytic phonics teaching on the reading and spelling ability of 10 year old boys and girls. *Reading and Writing*, 6, 1365–84. DOI: 10.1007/s11145-011-9323-x.

Johnston, R.S. and Watson, J. (2004) Accelerating the development of reading, spelling and phonemic awareness. *Reading and Writing*, 17(4), 327–57.

Johnston, R.S. and Watson, J. (2005) The effects of synthetic phonics teaching on reading and spelling attainment, a seven year longitudinal study. Edinburgh: Scottish Executive Education Department. http://www.scotland.gov.uk/library5/education/sptrs-00.asp (retrieved 27 August 2014).

Johnston, R.S., Watson, J.E. and Logan, S. (2009) Enhancing word reading, spelling and reading comprehension skills with synthetic phonics teaching: studies in Scotland and England. In C. Wood and V. Connelly (Eds) *Contemporary Perspectives on Reading and Spelling*. Abingdon: Routledge. pp221–38.

Macmillan Unit (2000) *The Group Reading Test II*. Windsor: NFER Nelson.

Mullis, I.V.S., Martin, M.O., Gonzalez, E.J. and Kennedy, A.M. (2003) *PIRLS 2001 International Report: IEA's Study of Reading Literacy Achievement in Primary Schools*. Chestnut Hill, MA: Boston College.

Naglieri, J.A. and Rojahn, J. (2001) Gender differences in Planning, Attention, Simultaneous, and Successive (PASS) cognitive processes and achievement. *Journal of Educational Psychology*, 93, 430–7.

Schonell, F.J. and Schonell, F.E. (1952) *Diagnostic and attainment testing* (2nd Edition). Edinburgh: Oliver and Boyd.

Skailand, D.B. (1971) A year comparison of four language units in teaching beginning reading. Paper presented at annual meeting of the American Educational Research Association, New York, 7 February.

Stuart, M., Dixon, M., Masterson, J. and Quinlan, P. (1998) Learning to read at home and at school. *British Journal of Educational Psychology*, 68, 3–14.

Torgerson, C.J., Brooks, G. and Hall, J. (2006) A Systematic Review of the Research Literature and use of phonics in the Teaching of Reading and Spelling. London: DfES. Research report RR711. http://dera.ioe.ac.uk/14791/1/RR711_.pdf (retrieved 18 March 2014).

Torgesen, J.K., Wagner, R.K., Rose, E., Lindamood, P., Conway, T. and Garvan, C. (1999) Preventing reading failure in children with phonological processing disabilities: group and individual responses to instruction. *Journal of Educational Psychology*, 91, 579–93.

Turner, M. (1990) *Sponsored reading failure. An object lesson*. Warlingham: IPSET Education Unit.

Watson, J. (1998) An investigation of the effects of phonics teaching on children's progress in reading and spelling. PhD thesis, University of St Andrews.

Wyse, D. and Styles, M. (2007) Synthetic phonics and the teaching of reading: the debate surrounding England's 'Rose Report'. *Literacy*, 41(1), 35–41. http://www.edalive.com/wp-content/uploads/2011/04/RoseEnquiryPhonicsPaperUKLA.pdf (retrieved 17 March 2014).

2
Phoneme awareness: what is it and what is its role in learning to read?

Learning objectives

In this chapter, you will learn that:

- the phoneme is the smallest unit of sound that changes a word's meaning;
- awareness of phonemes is related to letter knowledge and learning to read;
- research shows that when phoneme awareness is taught using letters it is more effective in developing reading skill than when it is taught on its own.

TEACHERS' STANDARDS

3. Demonstrate good subject and curriculum knowledge

What is a phoneme?

The phoneme is the smallest meaningful sound in our language; /c/ and /r/ are different phonemes, so exchanging one for the other turns the word 'cat' into 'rat', which changes the meaning. This is known as *phoneme substitution*; one phoneme is substituted for another, making a new word.

REFLECTIVE TASK

Task 1

How many phonemes do you think there are in spoken English?

See the end of the chapter for answers.

It is important to have a good understanding of phonemes, for both teachers and pupils, as the synthetic phonics method from the very start is based on blending sounds at the phoneme level in order to read unfamiliar words. However, young pre-readers do not have much spontaneous awareness of phonemes in spoken words.

REFLECTIVE TASK

Task 2

Complete the columns below. How many letters are there in each word? How many phonemes?

Words	Number of letters	Number of phonemes
fat		
book		
duck		
cuff		
shell		
scream		
which		
phone		
yacht		
bought		

See the end of the chapter for answers.

You will have seen that a phoneme can be represented by more than one letter. This is a test of *graphophonemic awareness* skills because you were looking at the printed words. Now try this out on a friend – speak the words (do not let them see this page), and then ask them how many phonemes there are in each word. When you test someone like this without showing them the printed words, you are testing their explicit *phoneme awareness* skills. Do not worry if you have made some mistakes in doing this exercise, research shows that skilled readers are not perfect at doing this task (Scarborough *et al.*, 1998) and adults can be trained to improve their graphophoneme awareness skills (Connelly, 2002). If you feel you need to work on this, we have provided another exercise in Appendix 1 to help you to develop your graphophonemic awareness skills. You can also see what errors are typically made by adults.

The association between phoneme awareness and learning to read

We know from many research studies that phoneme awareness ability is a good predictor of reading ability (for a review see Adams, 1990). The question arises as to whether children will have better reading skills later on if they are taught to segment spoken words into phonemes before they start to learn to read.

In order to test phoneme awareness in four-year-olds who cannot yet read you would ask them what the sounds are in a spoken word. Many children are puzzled by this abstract task; asked to tell us the sounds in 'ride', one child responded 'neigh'! However, in our work with pre-readers (Johnston *et al.*, 1996) we found that some four-year-olds in a nursery school were able to identify initial sounds in words, being able to say 'top' starts with the sound /t/. A few children could even tell us that the sounds are /t/ /o/ /p/. However, this ability to give the phonemes all through the word like this was only found in pre-readers who knew many of the letters of the alphabet. In fact, those children who knew no letters of the alphabet were very unlikely to be able to identify even one phoneme in a spoken word. Carroll (2004) also found that no four-year-old pre-reader had any phoneme awareness ability unless they knew at least one letter. Castles *et al.* (2011) have found that letter-sound learning enhances the development of phoneme awareness in pre-readers; when the children in the study learnt a small set of letter sounds, their phoneme awareness was subsequently better for those sounds than for the untrained ones. It was concluded that seeing the letters provided an extra memorial aid which was not available to the children who had only learnt the sounds.

Pre-readers often bring to the task of learning to read a number of proto-literacy skills; this includes not only some knowledge of the alphabet and a little phoneme aware-ness, but also the ability to read product names such as the names on sweet wrappers (which they cannot read in normal print). We found that both letter and phoneme aware-ness knowledge were predictive of product name reading ability in four-year-olds, but the most powerful predictor was letter knowledge (Johnston *et al.*, 1996). It is possible that early spontaneous phoneme awareness develops from a combination of letter-sound learning and the recognition of the print on enticing products such as sweets.

Phoneme awareness is known to be significantly associated with the ability to read nor-mal print, but Share *et al.* (1984) found that letter knowledge in young children starting school was just as predictive of later reading skill; he argued that these two skills are of equal importance and are co-requisites for learning to read. In fact, these two skills may interact, given the Castles *et al.* (2011) findings. As we will see later on, there is also evi-dence that teaching reading via the synthetic phonics method, where letter sounds are taught rapidly so that children can blend letter sounds in order to read unfamiliar words, is particularly effective in developing phoneme awareness.

These studies give us an indication that becoming aware of phonemes is not a skill that children acquire just through learning to speak; for pre-readers it is closely related to learning the alphabet. Even as adults we find it hard to think of phonemes without asso-ciating them with letters or graphemes; that is why graphophonemic awareness tasks, such as in Reflective Task 2, are difficult, as the spelling of the words disrupts our ability to think about the phonemes.

Port (2006), a linguist, proposes that phonemes are in fact a literacy-related concept. He argues that we use letters (especially the symbols in the International Phonetic Alphabet) to label speech sounds in English because we have been trained to read words in an alphabetic language. He points out that speech sounds can in fact be described in a num-ber of different ways, of which the phoneme level is just one; he argues that segmenting speech in this way comes naturally only to those who have learnt an alphabetic notation for writing down their language. However, he says that once we have learnt the letter-sound associations, then we have the impression that phonemes are the fundamental unit of the spoken language.

From large to small units: words, syllables, onset-rimes and phonemes

The phoneme is not the only level at which we can segment spoken words. They can be segmented into large units such as syllables (e.g. the two syllables in 'walk/ing'), and each syllable can be segmented into the smaller units of onset and rime (e.g. c/at, or st/op, or str/ong). The smallest unit of all is the phoneme level (s/t/r/o/ng).

As you will see from these examples, an onset is made up of the initial consonant or con-sonants of a syllable:

- the /c/ of c<u>at</u>
- the /st/ of <u>st</u>op
- the /str/ of <u>str</u>ong

whereas a rime consists of the vowel and the end part of the syllable:

- the /at/ of c<u>at</u>
- the /op/ of st<u>op</u>
- the /ong/ of str<u>ong</u>

REFLECTIVE TASK

Task 3

Complete the columns below, segmenting words into onsets, rimes, and phonemes.

Word	Onset	Rime	Phonemes
dog			
star			
sack			
crush			
snake			

See the end of the chapter for answers. Figure 2.1 shows a one-syllable word broken down at the onset-rime and then the phoneme level.

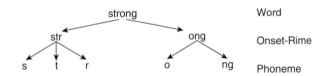

Figure 2.1 Segmenting words into onset-rimes and phonemes

Researchers use the overall term 'phonological awareness' to describe all these different levels of segmenting the spoken word, the smallest unit being the phoneme level (s/t/r/o/ng). To explain the various levels of segmentation we have to show you the words and letters in *print*, as in the figure above, but what we are talking about here is knowledge about the sounds in *spoken* words.

Do children's phonological skills develop from awareness of large units and then to progressively smaller units?

There is a view that it is necessary to teach children about larger units such as syllables and rhymes first and then later on to teach them about the smaller phoneme units. This comes from the idea that before they learn to read children find it easier to hear larger units of sounds, such as syllables and rhymes, and that small units such as phonemes are much harder for them to detect in spoken words.

This view is based on research that proposes that children show a developmental progression from first of all being aware of large units in speech, and then becoming aware of increasingly smaller units, showing the progression syllable->onset-rime->phoneme awareness (Treiman, 1987; Metsala and Walley, 1998). According to this view, what comes most easily to young children before learning to read is hearing syllables in words, as they find it easier to tap the syllables in words, e.g. two taps for 'cowboy', than to tap the phonemes in words, three taps for 'cat' (Liberman *et al.*, 1974). This progression is thought to be the same across all languages, and to be internally driven by an increasing vocabulary (Metsala and Walley, 1998). The argument is that as children learn more and more spoken words, they need to be able to make finer and finer discriminations in order to detect the differences between similar-sounding words. It is thought that early on children represent words at the whole word level, and then break them down into smaller elements as their vocabulary knowledge develops. As the catalyst for change is seen as being vocabulary development, it is thought that before starting reading tuition it is a good idea to expand children's spoken vocabularies in order to develop their phoneme awareness skills (Rose, 2006). However, this is an indirect and time-consuming method of developing phoneme awareness, so we need to be sure that this would be time well spent. It is of course highly desirable to develop children's vocabulary knowledge, but it should also be borne in mind that the reading of books is also a very effective way of achieving this.

Children develop awareness of small units earlier than previously thought

Gombert (1992) has alternatively argued that it is *language* development rather than *vocabulary* development that affects phonological development, which means that the characteristics of the child's native language will affect the process. Furthermore, according to his view there are also external factors that influence phonological development, of which a major one is learning to read. Duncan *et al.* (2006, Experiment 2) used a task where children aged from four upwards had to say which sound was the same in a pair of words. This is a more explicit test of phonological awareness than tapping the number of sounds in words. The children identified syllables, initial phonemes or rimes in lists of pairs of spoken words, after hearing a puppet demonstrate the phonological unit required for each list. Duncan *et al.* (2006) found that four-year-old non-reading French children were indeed better at identifying syllables than phonemes and rimes at this age, but English-speaking children actually identified phonemes a little better than syllables and rimes. Furthermore, the ability to identify an initial shared phoneme increased greatly in the English-speaking children once they started to learn to read using a phonic approach at the age of five. The French children's ability to identify phonemes also increased greatly when they started to learn to read at the age of six using a phonic approach. These findings point to learning to read as being a very important factor in developing phoneme awareness.

In one of our studies (Johnston *et al.* 1996) we expected, because of the prevailing view that rhyme skills develop before phoneme awareness skills, that preschool children would be good at producing rhymes compared to saying the phonemes in spoken words. However, on average these four-year-olds only scored 24% correct in a task where we asked them, for example, for a word that rhymed with 'hop'. In fact, we noticed that they often produced an alliterative response instead, saying a word beginning with the same sound, e.g. 'hat'. Furthermore, in a task where they had to say what sounds there were in spoken words, the score was 23% correct for the first phoneme in words, e.g. saying that 'top' starts with /t/. Thus their level of performance on this task was very similar to their performance on the rhyme task.

Phonological awareness training and *Letters and Sounds*

Letters and Sounds (DfES, 2007, Chapter 4) recommends that you develop children's phonological awareness skills in Phase 1, before starting a synthetic phonics programme in Phase 2. Indeed, not only does *Letters and Sounds* recommend that children orally sound and blend phonemes to produce words (and to segment phonemes in spoken words) before they get started on learning to read via a synthetic phonics programme, they propose that these activities should be continued throughout Phase 2. It is important to consider therefore how children become aware of phonemes all through the word. The studies cited above have shown pre-school children to have quite surprisingly good awareness of the phonemes at the beginning of words (i.e. onsets), but most of them are not very adept at giving the phonemes in other positions in words. It may seem logical to conclude from this that training children in blending and segmenting phonemes in spoken words without showing letters would be beneficial for developing their phoneme awareness skills all through the word and so speed up learning to read. However, after carrying out a major review of the literature, Castles and Coltheart (2004) have concluded that no study has established that phoneme awareness training on its own assists reading development, whereas there is overwhelming evidence that when phoneme awareness is taught in the context of letters it has a positive effect on learning to read. They argue that only a few studies are suggestive of a causal link between phoneme awareness training without letters and improved literacy skills, and that these studies are open to question because they were, for example, carried out on children who may have had some knowledge of the alphabet and/or were at school and already learning to read.

Leaving aside Castles and Coltheart's (2004) methodological criticisms of the studies that claim to find phoneme awareness training on its own to be beneficial in developing reading skill, it is possible to assess how useful training phoneme awareness alone is compared to learning about phonemes at the same time as learning about letters. Ehri *et al.* (2001), in a meta-analysis of 52 studies for the US National Reading Panel, showed that when phoneme awareness was taught using letters this was statistically more effective in developing reading skill than when it was taught without letters.

It is interesting to look in detail at some UK studies that have examined the effects of phonological awareness training on children's reading skills. Hatcher *et al.* (1994) found that seven-year-old poor readers receiving a phonological awareness training programme in a separate session to their reading lesson did indeed improve their performance on a test of phoneme awareness, but their reading skills were no better than a group that did not get this intervention. Similarly, we found in our study in Clackmannanshire (Johnston and Watson, 2004) that normal school entrants learning to read by an analytic phonics programme scored 17% correct (up from 4.5%) on a test of all-through-the-word phoneme awareness at the end of the programme. A second group had an analytic phonics programme that was supplemented by daily lessons on blending and segmenting phonemes without using letters and print, and they scored 35% correct (up from 2.7%); this was better than that of the first group, but this difference was not statistically significant. However, a third group was taught to read by a synthetic phonics method where the children learnt to blend and segment phonemes all through the word in the context of letters and print. Their score on the phoneme awareness task was 4.1% correct before they did the synthetic phonics programme, and 65% correct at the end of the programme. Their performance was significantly better than that of the first and second group. Of particular interest is the fact that the second group had training on phonemes all through the word *without letters*, but were found to have nearly half the level of phoneme awareness of the synthetic phonics group, who had had similar training *with letters*. These data are shown in Figure 2.2.

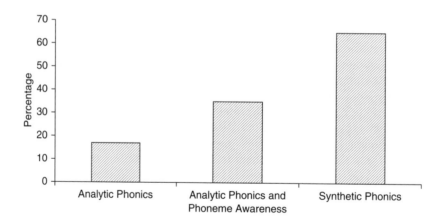

Figure 2.2   Phonemic awareness ability in March of first year at school, Clackmannanshire Study

Furthermore, what is really important is how well the children read. At the end of the training, the synthetic phonics group read seven months ahead of the two analytic phonics groups, and spelt eight to nine months ahead. The analytic phonics group that had a supplementary phoneme awareness training programme did not read or spell better than the group that just did analytic phonics, despite having higher levels of phoneme awareness ability. These findings support the conclusion that Ehri *et al.* (2001) drew from their meta-analysis – it is much better to learn about phonemes in the context of letters and print. Phonemes are a very abstract concept, but when taught with letters and print children have concrete visual representations of the sounds and these support their learning.

A SUMMARY OF **KEY POINTS**

➢ Studies have shown that contrary to the idea that children at first become aware of large units such as rhymes, and only later become aware of smaller units such as phonemes, preschool children's phoneme awareness skills are as good as their rhyme skills.

➢ Children's preschool phoneme awareness ability is associated with early proto-literacy skills, e.g. knowledge of letters of the alphabet and ability to recognise environmental print such as the product names on sweet wrappers.

➢ Children learn phoneme awareness better in the context of letters and print compared to learning without this concrete visual support.

➢ Children who learn phoneme awareness using letters and print develop significantly better reading and spelling skills than those who have separate phoneme awareness training.

REFLECTIVE TASK

Task 1 answer

The total number of distinct sounds in spoken English vary with accent, but it is generally agreed that there are 40+.

If you answered 26 to this question, you were thinking of the number of letters in the alphabet. We do not have a letter for each sound in English, which is why we have to double up letters, particularly for vowels, e.g. 'coat', 'feet'. Spellings like 'oa' and 'ee' are called vowel digraphs. There are also consonant digraphs, e.g. 'ship', 'chop'. In both cases we use two letters to stand for one sound.

REFLECTIVE TASK

Task 2 answers

Words	Number of letters	Number of phonemes	Phonemes
fat	3	3	/f/ /a/ /t/
book	4	3	/b/ /oo/ k/
duck	4	3	/d/ /u/ /ck/
cuff	4	3	/c/ /u/ ff/
shell	5	3	/sh/ /e/ /ll/
scream	6	5	/s/ /c/ /r/ /ea/ /m/
which	5	3	/wh/ /i/ /ch/
phone	5	3	/ph/ /o/ /n/
yacht	5	3	/y/ /ach/ /t/
bought	6	3	/b/ /ough/ /t/

REFLECTIVE TASK

Task 3 answers

Word	Onset	Rime	Phonemes
dog	d-	-og	/d/ /o/ /g/
star	st-	-ar	/s/ /t/ /a/ /r/
sack	s-	-ack	/s/ /a/ /ck/
crush	cr-	-ush	/c/ /r/ /u/ /sh/
snake	sn-	-ake	/s/ /n/ /a/ /k/

REFERENCES REFERENCES **REFERENCES** REFERENCES **REFERENCES** REFERENCES

Adams, M.J. (1990) *Beginning to read: Learning and thinking about print*. London: MIT.

Carroll, J.M. (2004) Letter knowledge precipitates phoneme segmentation, but not phoneme invariance. *Journal of Research in Reading*, 27(3), 212–25.

Castles, A. and Coltheart, M. (2004) Is there a causal link from phonological awareness to success in learning to read? *Cognition*, 91, 77–111.

Castles, A., Wilson, K. and Coltheart, M. (2011) Early orthographic knowledge influences on phonemic awareness tasks: Evidence from a preschool training study. *Journal of Experimental Child Psychology*, 108(1), 203–10.

Connelly, V. (2002) Graphophonemic awareness, in adults after instruction in phonic generalisations. *Learning and Instruction*, 12(6), 627–49.

DfES (2007) *Letters and Sounds*. London: DfES. https://www.gov.uk/government/publications/letters-and-sounds (retrieved 27 August 2014).

Duncan, L.G., Cole, P., Seymour, P.H.K. and Magnan, A. (2006) Differing sequences of metaphonological development in English and French. *Journal of Child Language*, 33, 369–99.

Ehri, L.C., Nunes, S.R., Willows, D.M., Schuster, B.V., Yaghoub-Zadeh, Z. and Shanahan, T. (2001) Phonemic awareness instruction helps children learn to read: Evidence from the National Reading Panel's meta-analysis. *Reading Research Quarterly*, 36, 250–87.

Gombert, J.E. (1992) *Metalinguistic Development*. London: Harvester Wheatsheaf.

Hatcher, P.J. and Hulme, C. and Ellis, A.W. (1994) Ameliorating early reading failure by integrating the teaching of reading and phonological skills: the phonological linkage hypothesis. *Child Development*, 65, 41–57.

Johnston, R.S., Anderson, M. and Holligan, C. (1996) Knowledge of the alphabet and explicit awareness of phonemes in pre-readers: the nature of the relationship. *Reading and Writing*, 8, 217–34.

Johnston, R.S. and Watson, J. (2004) Accelerating the development of reading, spelling and phonemic awareness. *Reading and Writing*, 17(4), 327–57.

Liberman, I.Y., Shankweiler, D., Fischer, F.W. and Carter, B. (1974) Explicit syllable and phoneme segmentation in the young child. *Journal of Experimental Child Psychology*, 18, 201–12.

Metsala, J.L. and Walley, A.C. (1998) Spoken vocabulary growth and segmental restructuring of lexical representations: precursors to phonemic awareness and early reading ability. In J.L. Metsala and L.C. Ehri (Eds) *Word recognition in beginning literacy*. Mahwah, NJ: Erlbaum. pp89–120.

Port, R.F. (2006) The graphical basis of phones and phonemes. In M. Munro and O. Bohn (Eds) *Second Language Speech Learning: The Role of Language Experience in Speech Perception and Production*. Amsterdam: Benjamins. pp349–65. http://www.cs.indiana.edu/~port/pubs.html (retrieved 12 March 2014).

Rose, J. (2006) *Independent Review of the Teaching of Early Reading: Final Report*. Nottingham: DfES. http://webarchive.nationalarchives.gov.uk/20100408085953/http://standards.dcsf.gov.uk/phonics/rosereview/ (retrieved 27 August 2014).

Scarborough, H.S., Ehri, L.C., Olson, R.K. and Fowler, A. (1998) The Fate of Phonemic Awareness Beyond the Elementary Schools Years. *Scientific Studies of Reading*, 2, 115–43.

Share, D.L., Jorm, A.F., Maclean, R. and Matthews, R. (1984) Sources of individual differences in reading acquisition. *Journal of Educational Psychology*, 76, 1309–24.

Treiman, R. (1987) On the relationship between phonological awareness and literacy. *Cahiers de Psychologie Cognitive*, 7, 524–9.

3
How does reading develop?

Learning objectives

In this chapter, you will learn that:

- the Primary National Strategy has adopted the Simple View of Reading;
- according to the Simple View, reading is composed of two processes: recognising the printed word and understanding spoken language;
- sight word recognition becomes increasing underpinned by sound information as reading skill develops.

TEACHERS' STANDARDS

3. Demonstrate good subject and curriculum knowledge

The Simple View of Reading

It is obvious that we cannot read if we are not able to recognise the words on the printed page. If this page was printed in the Greek alphabet many of us would not be able to say what even one word was, let alone get the full meaning. So there are two aspects to reading – recognising the words and getting meaning from the sentences. Although most children starting school cannot recognise the printed word, they understand much of what is said to them. That is, they start school with linguistic comprehension. If they learn to read a few words after starting school, such as 'the', 'cat', 'sat', 'on', 'the', 'mat', understanding the resulting sentence would easily be within their comprehension abilities, and they would be able to draw a picture of this for you to show that they understood it.

Although reading is a very complex skill, according to Gough and Tunmer (1986) in their Simple View of Reading it can be reduced to two components:

- recognising and decoding printed words;
- linguistic comprehension, the ability to understand spoken language.

Studies have shown that separate measures of word recognition (decoding) and linguistic comprehension together give a good account of how well children comprehend what they read (Hoover and Gough, 1990). This means that, by and large, *reading comprehension ability* (R) can be predicted by multiplying *decoding* (D) and *linguistic comprehension ability* (C) together:

$$R = D \times C.$$

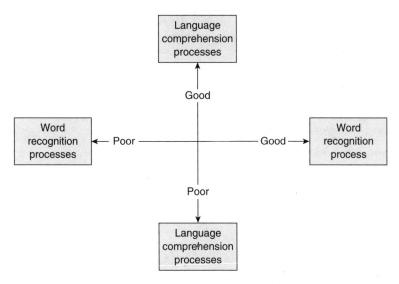

Figure 3.1 The Simple View of Reading

Source: Rose, 2006, p77

Despite this there has been a view that learning to decode is not important (Goodman, 1973; Smith, 1982), and this view has been very influential in the English-speaking world. Thirty or so years ago it was believed that when a skilled adult reads he or she does not take in all the printed words on the page, and gets meaning largely by getting the gist of what is written. However, since then it has been shown by studying eye movements that we do indeed sample pretty much every word on the page. Guessing from context is what *unskilled* readers do, because of their inability to recognise all the words (Stanovich, 1980). It does not mean that it is a good way to read or that we should teach children to do that. It is actually quite hard to get a missing word by guessing, e.g. 'Jack went for a ......'. This could be a walk, a swim or even a pizza! Children's reading progresses much better if they have a method for working out what an unfamiliar word is, rather than guessing, looking for picture cues, or asking the teacher. This means that the flow of reading is not broken up, which helps children to get the meaning from what they are reading. In a study where two groups were matched on decoding ability, in which one group of children had systematic instruction in phonics and the other learnt to read by a comprehension approach, reading comprehension was actually better in the phonics-taught group (Connelly *et al.*, 2001).

Children can have problems in either word recognition or listening comprehension, or indeed both areas. There is much evidence that dyslexic children have a primary problem in recognising the printed word, and indeed one influential definition of dyslexia is that it is 'a specific language-based disorder of constitutional origin characterised by difficulties in single word decoding' (Lyon, 1995, p9). However, there are also children who have adequate word recognition abilities, but have difficulty in comprehending what they read (Cain and Oakhill, 2004).

The Primary National Strategy (2006) in England represented the simple view of reading in a chart like the one above (see Figure 3.1). A child may have poor word recognition skills, but despite this if a text is read out to them that child may show good understanding of the meaning. However, another child may have good word recognition skills and yet have poor understanding of a text when it is read out loud. Another child may have poor word recognition skills and poor comprehension of a text when it is read out loud. Finally a child can be good in both areas. These are of course the extremes on these dimensions, and a child's performance may lie at any point on the continuum, but in showing the extremes the point is that when you are teaching your pupils to read, they will not necessarily progress equally fast in both areas. Separating out these two dimensions draws our attention to the fact that children's progress in these two areas needs to be monitored and assessed, so that if they fall behind they can receive extra help to enable them to catch up.

The purpose of introducing synthetic phonics teaching early on in primary schooling is to eradicate as far as possible the problems children have in recognising the printed word, in order to allow more time in the curriculum for developing comprehension of what they read.

How do children learn to recognise the printed word?

We know that, as skilled readers, when we move our eyes from left to right across the page we rapidly gain the meaning of each word, and so make sense of the text. But how did we come to be able to recognise the words?

For some children, a few exposures to a printed word, its pronunciation and its meaning are enough to secure the word in memory. It is unlikely that these children are just using the visual pattern the word makes; many words are visually similar because we only have 26 letters in the alphabet. Young children who think that recognising words means looking at the shape will learn some words, but as they learn more words they will soon find it difficult to distinguish them from similar looking ones. To varying extents (the amount depending on the method by which they have been taught) children learning to read in English will use information from the sounds that the letters represent. We know that some children can work out the alphabetic code for themselves. Children learning to read using the official scheme in New Zealand, where only the names of the letters of the alphabet are taught, can read 'made up' or 'nonwords', such as 'poast', that they have never seen before (Johnston and Thompson, 1989). However, they read nonwords less well than phonics-taught children, and a substantial number of children in New Zealand join the Reading Recovery programme at the age of six, as they need extra help with reading.

Before looking at phonics teaching in later chapters, we need to look at what we know about how children's ability to recognise words develops. When children start school their cognitive and perceptual skills are still developing and they are unlikely to be able to recognise words in the way an adult would.

A model of sight word reading development

One very influential model of reading development (Ehri, 2005) encompasses the thinking of other major theorists, and has been tested extensively over a long period of time. This

Table 3.1 Ehri's Model of Reading Development

	Main characteristics of word reading	Examples
Pre-alphabetic phase	Child reads by salient visual cues and does not look at letters	Reads 'Xepsi' as 'Pepsi' if presented within its distinctive logo
Partial alphabetic phase	Child uses some letter sound information	Reads 'tin' as 'toy', reads 'jail' as 'jewel'
Full alphabetic phase	Child makes connections between letters and sounds all through the words, including vowels	Reads an unfamiliar word, e.g. 'dog', by converting letters into sounds all through the word
Consolidated alphabetic phase	Child recognises large elements such as morphemes	Recognises 'dance' and 'ed', so can read 'danced' on the basis of these two units

model looks closely at the development of sight word reading, and how that changes over time (see Table 3.1).

When teaching children who have got going with reading, it is evident that they know some words by 'sight', that is, they look at them and instantly know what they are. Less familiar words have to be worked out, either by blending the sequence of letter sounds, via a synthetic phonics approach, or perhaps by making analogies with other known words, for example reasoning that 'date' looks like 'late' but starts with 'd'. We know quite a lot about phonic or phonological approaches to reading, but relatively little about how 'sight' word reading is carried out. It has been thought for a long time that sight word reading in a skilled adult reader is largely visual, e.g. based on letter patterns or perhaps even word shape, with little or no information about letter sounds being activated. Ehri reasoned that if children need to use letter sound information while they are learning to read unfamiliar words, it would be surprising for that just to wither away as they become more skilled. She proposes that even when an adult is seeing a familiar word, information about its visual appearance, meaning and sounds are all likely to be activated, although the sound information would not be actually needed to pronounce familiar words.

Ehri proposes that sight word reading changes as reading skill increases. She suggests that in the very earliest stages of recognising print, children do indeed take a very visual approach, but that as their reading skill progresses their word recognition becomes more and more underpinned by the sounds.

One way to examine developmental change is to describe phases or stages in the development of the skill. Development is complex and dynamic, whereas when we describe stages they sound simple and static. We use stage theories as a way of getting a handle on the complexities of how skills are developing, taking a snapshot of what is going on in a child's reading at one particular point in time. When we do put children's reading under the microscope in this way, we find there are great similarities in what children are doing, even though as teachers what you will see looks more like diversity. The approaches taken by children in a class may look diverse to the teacher, as if they are learning to read in a different way, but they are generally at a slightly different point on the same developmental pathway.

Ehri has studied this developmental pathway by examining phases in reading development, looking at how printed words are being stored in memory at a particular point in time.

Pre-alphabetic phase

Here Ehri found the approach taken to be very visual. Children focus on a salient visual cue in the word, or even something external to the word, like a thumbprint! Ehri found that early on children could 'read' a word like Pepsi (when presented within its distinctive logo), and even if a letter was changed so it read Xepsi, many of the children would identify it as Pepsi. This was despite the children knowing 60% of the names of the letters of the alphabet. The logos surrounding such words do act like the thumbprint, that is, it is an external or contextual cue that draws the child's attention from the actual print. It has been found, however, that nursery children do have some success in identifying words like 'Smarties' if the word is presented in its distinctive print, but with the logo information removed. However, the children generally cannot recognise such a word when it is presented in normal print (Johnston *et al.*, 1996). So children in this phase generally use visual cues to recognise words even if they know some letter names or sounds, as they do not know how to use that information. We can conclude that preschool children are very aware of print in their environment, especially when it helps them identify a favourite chocolate bar, but the way they recognise it is a long way from the alphabetical reading they develop once they start to learn to read at school.

Partial alphabetic phase

This phase emerges when children can relate letter sounds to printed words. However, at this stage they cannot work all the way through the letter sounds in words in order from left to right. You can get a feel for how a child is dealing with print through the errors he or she makes. For example, if the child can recognise the word 'toy', when faced with the word 'tin' they may fix on the 't' and think they are seeing the word 'toy'. So this is a partial alphabetic approach. This type of error is very common when children are learning by an analytic phonics approach, if they are at the stage where letter sounds are taught only at the beginning of words. As their reading skill progresses, children may recognise the beginning and end letters, reading the word 'jail' as 'jewel'. Again, such an approach may be facilitated by analytic phonics teaching, which follows up teaching letter sounds in the initial position of words by drawing children's attention to the role of letter sounds at the ends of words. So in this phase sight word reading is becoming more closely tied to the sounds of the letter in the words.

Full alphabetic phase

In this phase children are able to make connections between letters and sounds all through the word. To be able to read like this, children need to convert the vowel letters into sounds. In analytic phonics, towards the end of the first year at school simple vowels, as in words like 'c<u>a</u>t', 'd<u>o</u>g', 't<u>a</u>p', are taught in the middle of words. This means that faced with an unfamiliar CVC word, the children can work out for themselves how to read it. This is particularly so if they are taught to sound each letter in sequence from left to right and blend the sounds together. So faced with an unfamiliar word, they can work out the sounds for each letter, e.g. /p/ /a/ /t/, and then blend them to find that the word is 'pat'. This approach is taught right from the start in synthetic phonics.

So far we have been talking about letter–sound correspondences, but written English often represents sounds with more than one letter. Our spelling system is largely phoneme based. What is a phoneme? A phoneme is the smallest unit of sound that changes a word's meaning. So we can change the spoken word 'cat' into 'rat' just by changing the first phoneme, which in this case means changing a single letter. Other phonemes are not spelt so simply, and can be made up of several letters. For example, we write the sound /sh/, and the long /o/ sound in 'coat', with two letters. 'Sh' is a consonant digraph and 'oa' is a vowel digraph; these are graphemes which represent the spoken phonemes. However, some words in English are irregularly spelt, and are not amenable to such a straightforward mapping between graphemes and phonemes. For a long time it was thought that these words were read visually. However, even the word 'yacht' provides some guide to pronunciation through its initial and final letters. We know that children probably do use letter–sound connections even with these words, as there is such a high association between children's ability to read regular and irregular (common exception) words (Stuart and Masterson, 1992).

This phase is a very enabling one for children to reach, as they now have the means to teach themselves how to pronounce a lot of the new words they meet. But as skilled readers we know that when we have worked out what a word is, we do not need to go through the laborious process of decoding it each time we see it; we recognise it instantly.

Consolidated alphabetic phase

This brings us to the final phase of Ehri's model. Ehri argues that we develop recognition for larger elements such as morphemes, that is, meaning-based units. For example 'danced' is composed of the root morpheme 'dance' and the grammatical morpheme '-ed'. We also recognise onsets, which can be single phonemes (e.g. 'c' in 'cat', 'sh' as in 'shop'), or several phonemes (and therefore several graphemes) such as 'str' in 'string', and we also recognise rimes, such as 'ing' in 'string'. Once we can read the word 'string', when we meet words like 'king' and 'thing' we can recognise the 'ing' segment as a whole unit. So when we meet an unfamiliar word, we may not need to go to the grapheme level to work out how to pronounce it; we may be able to use larger chunks. There will also be one-syllable words that are so familiar that we can recognise them instantly on sight, without making analogies with other words. However, Ehri does not think that we ever come to a stage where we read words purely visually, without other information becoming available. That is, however familiar we are with a word, when we recognise it we draw from our memory its meaning, its whole word pronunciation, and all the connections between letters and sounds (e.g. its connections to letters at the phoneme, onset and rime levels). What we do not need to do any longer is laboriously build up the pronunciation of the word from the graphemes by blending their sounds or by making an analogy with another word. So this final phase is also sight word reading, but it is 'paved with phonological information' (Ehri, 1992, p114).

REFLECTIVE TASK

Task 1

Phases of reading development

Observing children showing the following patterns of reading, in which column would you place each child? Enter a number for each child. They may be in more than one phase, pick the most likely one.

1. Child reads 'Ribena' on the bottle but cannot read it in normal print.
2. Child reads 'kicking' without sounding and blending but has not seen this combination of morphemes ('kick' and 'ing') before.
3. Child reads 'Kit-Kat' on a packet and can sound and blend 'kitkat' when it is presented in normal print.
4. Child reads 'pill' for the word 'pail'.

Pre-alphabetic	Partial alphabetic	Full alphabetic	Consolidated alphabetic

See the end of the chapter for answers.

Synthetic phonics and phases in reading development

Typically in a synthetic phonics programme, children just starting school learn four letter sounds (three consonants and a vowel), and then are shown words built up from those letter sounds. For example, in the space of a few days they learn the letters 's', 'a', 't', 'p' and then when shown unfamiliar words, such as 'at', 'sat', 'pat', 'tap', 'nap', taps', 'pats', they can blend the letter sounds to find out what the words are. This gives children a lot of independence in reading from very early on. This means that there need not be a partial alphabetic phase where a child tries to read words by saying another word start-ing with the same letter, such as saying 'toy' when the word is 'tap', or by identifying the beginning and end letters, saying 'top' for 'tap'. They use a full alphabetic approach right from the start, taking account of letter sounds all through unfamiliar words. This means that when faced with an unfamiliar word they have a strategy to work out what it is for themselves, so they do not need to look at a picture for cues, or try to guess what it is from the rest of the sentence. Once they have seen a word a few times and worked out what it is, they may recognise it on subsequent occasions without having to build up the pronunciation. This is a big advantage when reading for meaning, as the child can focus on getting meaning from the text, rather than expending a lot of effort on working out what the words are.

Ehri (2005) proposes that the partial alphabetic phase occurs in children who do not have full knowledge of the alphabet, and who lack phonemic segmentation skill. Research sug-gests that many poor readers are partial alphabetic readers (Romani *et al.*, 2005), and there is evidence that very bright poor readers in particular take a rather visual approach to reading (Johnston and Morrison, 2007). This suggests that such children are not taking full advantage of the alphabetic code underlying English spelling. Given that with the synthetic phonics method there are very few underachievers (Johnston and Watson, 2005), it is likely that this method of teaching inhibits children at risk of reading failure from developing a partial alphabetic approach to reading. Children who start school with little or no phoneme or rhyme awareness are considered to be at risk of reading failure. Around 40% of the children in the Clackmannanshire Study started school lacking these skills, but nevertheless they made very good progress: by the end of the second year at school they read words around eight months ahead of chronological age (Johnston and Watson, 2004). As the synthetic phonics approach not only developed their letter-sound knowledge and phonemic awareness skills, but also taught them how to apply these skills all through words right from the start, it is likely that they were able to bypass the partial alphabetic reading phase altogether and progress rapidly to the full and consolidated alphabetic reading phases.

A SUMMARY OF **KEY POINTS**

➤ The Primary National Strategy in England adopted the Simple View of Reading. This model proposes that decoding printed words (D) is a separate skill which, together with linguistic comprehension ability (C), gives a good account of a child's reading comprehension (R), that is R = D x C.

➤ Children having problems with either decoding or linguistic comprehension will have problems with reading comprehension.

➤ Children who are taught phonics use the sounds of the letters of the alphabet to derive the pronunciation of unfamiliar words.

➤ In analytic phonics children learn to recognise words by sight and then learn about letter sounds at the beginning, at the end and then finally in the middle of words. It can take a year to start to learn to use letter sounds all through an unfamiliar word to find its pronunciation.

➤ In synthetic phonics, children learn to blend the letter sounds all through an unfamiliar word to get its pronunciation right from the start of reading tuition.

➤ Ehri's model of sight word reading development describes four phases in reading development: 1) pre-alphabetic, 2) partial alphabetic, 3) full alphabetic and 4) consolidated alphabetic.

➤ When children learn to recognise words using a synthetic phonics method, they are developing a full alphabetic phase approach, by-passing the previous three phases.

REFLECTIVE TASK

Task 1 answers

Pre-alphabetic	Partial alphabetic	Full alphabetic	Consolidated alphabetic
1	4	3	2

REFERENCES REFERENCES **REFERENCES** REFERENCES REFERENCES REFERENCES

Cain, K. and Oakhill, J. (2004) Reading comprehension difficulties. In T. Nunes, and P. Bryant (Eds) *Handbook of Children's Literacy*. Dordrecht: Kluwer Academic Publishers.

Connelly, V., Johnston, R.S. and Thompson, G.B. (2001) The effects of phonics instruction on the reading comprehension of beginning readers. *Reading and Writing*, 14, 423–57.

Ehri, L.C. (1992) Reconceptualizing the development of sight word reading and its relationship to recoding. In P. Gough, L. Ehri and R. Treiman (Eds) *Reading Acquisition*. Hillsdale, NJ: Erlbaum. pp107–43.

Ehri, L.C. (2005) Development of Sight Word Reading: Phases and Findings. In M.J. Snowling and C. Hulme (Eds) *The Science of Reading: A handbook*. Oxford: Blackwell. pp135–54.

Goodman, K.S. (1973) The 13th easy way to make learning to read difficult: A reaction to Gleitman and Rozin. *Reading Research Quarterly*, 8, 484–93.

Gough, P.B. and Tunmer, W.E. (1986) Decoding, reading and reading disability. *Remedial Special Education*, 7, 6–10.

Hoover, W.A. and Gough, P.B. (1990) The Simple View of Reading. *Reading and Writing*, 2, 127–60.

Johnston, R.S., Anderson, M. and Holligan, C. (1996) Knowledge of the alphabet and explicit awareness of phonemes in pre-readers: the nature of the relationship. *Reading and Writing*, 8, 217–34.

Johnston, R.S. and Morrison, M. (2007) Towards a resolution of inconsistencies in the phonological deficit theory of reading disorders: phonological reading difficulties are more severe in high IQ poor readers. *Journal of Learning Disabilities*, 40, 66–79.

Johnston, R.S. and Thompson, G.B. (1989) Is dependence on phonological information in children's reading a product of instructional approach? *Journal of Experimental Child Psychology*, 48, 131–45.

Johnston, R.S. and Watson, J. (2004) Accelerating the development of reading, spelling and phonemic awareness. *Reading and Writing*, 17(4), 327–57.

Johnston, R.S. and Watson, J. (2005) The effects of synthetic phonics teaching on reading and spelling attainment, a seven-year longitudinal study. Edinburgh: Scottish Executive Education Department. http://www.scotland.gov.uk/library5/education/sptrs-00.asp (retrieved 27 August 2014).

Lyon, G.R. (1995) Toward a definition of dyslexia. *Annals of Dyslexia*, 45, 3–27.

Primary National Strategy (2006) *The Primary Framework for literacy and mathematics: core position papers underpinning the renewal of guidance for literacy teaching and mathematics*. London: DfES. http://www.niched.org/docs/the%20primary%20framework.pdf (retrieved 27 August 2014).

Romani, C., Olson, A. and DiBetta, A.M. (2005) Spelling Disorders. In M.J. Snowling and C. Hulme (Eds) *The Science of Reading: A handbook*. Oxford: Blackwell. pp431–47.

Rose, J. (2006) *Independent Review of the Teaching of Early Reading*. Nottingham: DfES. http://webarchive.nationalarchives.gov.uk/20100408085953/http://standards.dcsf.gov.uk/phonics/rosereview/ (retrieved 27 August 2014).

Smith, F. (1982) *Understanding Reading*. New York: Hilt, Rinehart and Winston.

Stanovich, K. (1980) Toward an interactive-compensatory model of individual differences in the development of reading fluency. *Reading Research Quarterly*, 16, 32–71.

Stuart, M. and Masterson, J. (1992) Patterns of reading and spelling in 10 year old children related to prereading phonological abilities. *Journal of Experimental Child Psychology*, 54, 168–87.

4
Teaching synthetic phonics: the National Curriculum and an overview of *Letters and Sounds*

Learning objectives

In this chapter, you will:

- gain knowledge of the National Curriculum's statutory requirements for the teaching of reading and spelling in England;
- gain an understanding of the government programme *Letters and Sounds*;
- see an overview of a typical *Letters and Sounds* phonics lesson;
- gain an understanding of the phases of phonic development outlined in *Letters and Sounds*.

TEACHERS' STANDARDS

3. Demonstrate good subject and curriculum knowledge
4. Plan and teach well structured lessons
5. Adapt teaching to respond to the strengths and needs of all pupils

The statutory requirements in the National Curriculum (England)

The new National Curriculum sets out the framework for teaching in Key Stages 1 and 2 in England (DfE, 2013), and came into force in 2014. What is relevant here is the programme of study for English in Key Stage 1, where the reading and spelling skills to be taught at each stage, and the methods to be used, are described in detail.

Pupils should be taught that letter sound correspondences underpin the reading of all words, and should not be taught to read using multiple cues

On page 19 it says that in Year 1 teachers should build on work from the Early Years Foundation Stage, so that children can sound and blend unfamiliar words using their phonic knowledge. It says that pupils should understand that letter–sound correspondences underpin the reading and spelling of *all* words; that is, unfamiliar words should not be taught by sight without reference to the letter–sound correspondences. As this applies to *all* unfamiliar words, not only should high frequency regularly spelt words not be taught by sight, but neither should common exception (i.e. 'tricky') words. It lists the statutory requirements for word reading, saying that 'pupils should be taught to read accurately by blending sounds in unfamiliar words containing GPCs that have been taught' and to 'read common exception words, noting unusual correspondences between spelling and sound and where these occur in the word' (p20).

It also says on page 20 that children should be taught to 'read aloud accurately books that are consistent with their developing phonic knowledge and that do not require them to use other strategies to work out words'. This means that children should not be taught to decode words by looking at picture cues and/or guessing from context. It also gives further guidance that although children may not know the meaning of all the words they decode, this approach provides 'opportunities not only for pupils to develop confidence in their decoding skills, but also for teachers to explain the meaning and thus develop pupils' vocabulary'.

Pupils should be taught to segment all spoken words for spelling

The spelling appendix (p50) has the statutory requirement that spelling should be taught by 'segmenting spoken words into sounds before choosing graphemes to represent the sounds'; this was the method used in Reception, which should be revised in Year 1. This includes common exception words: 'Pupils' attention should be drawn to the grapheme–phoneme correspondences that do and do not fit in with what has been taught so far' (p54). Even after Key Stage 1, phonic knowledge should similarly continue to underpin spelling (p49): 'teachers should still draw pupils' attention to GPCs that do and do not fit in with what has been taught so far'. This means that spelling should not be taught by sight, using a 'look, say, cover, write and check' approach.

There was similar guidance from the Department for Education (2012) in the document 'Criteria for assuring high-quality phonic work', where it says that 'children should not be expected to use strategies such as whole-word recognition and/or cues from context, grammar, or pictures'. Of course this does not mean that children do not use context to gain an understanding of text, it means that children should not be taught to use context or picture cues in order to decode unfamiliar words. This is the approach recommended in the government programme *Letters and Sounds* (DfES, 2007), which we will describe in more detail later on in this chapter; however, these recommendations have now been made statutory. The reason for this is that these other strategies undermine the synthetic phonics approach.

Current teaching practice

The question arises as to whether children in England are being taught according to these statutory requirements.

Our study of phonics teaching methods in England

We have carried out a study looking at how phonics teaching was implemented in an area of northern England (Johnston *et al.*, in preparation). We studied 213 children who sat the government's Phonics Check at the end of Year 1 in 2012 (at the end of their second year at school); see Chapter 8 for more details of the Phonics Check. The expected level of performance was a score of 32 or above; Table 4.1 shows how well the children did. We found that 56.5% of children reached the expected level at the end of Year 1: 45% of the boys and 68% of the girls. The national average was 58% of children reaching the expected level.

Table 4.1 Mean Year 1 Phonics Check scores in 2012

Gender	Phonics Check scores out of 40
Girls N = 108	32.16
Boys N = 105	27.04
Total N = 213	29.63

We asked the Reception and Year 1 teachers of these children to fill in questionnaires to find out how the children had been taught phonics. We also looked at the pace of phonics teaching in the schools, according to the government's Phonics Phases (Primary National Strategy, 2006). These phases will be described in more detail later on in the chapter, but they are summarised here. Phase 1 relates to nursery teaching, where children learn to orally blend and segment phonemes in spoken words without the use of letters. In Phase 2, starting in Reception, children learn the sounds for 19 letters of the alphabet, and the core synthetic phonics method is introduced whereby they learn to sound and blend these letters for reading and to segment words containing these sounds for spelling. In Phase 3 the rest of the letters of the alphabet are taught for blending and segmenting, as well as some vowel and consonant digraphs, and in Phase 4 the children learn adjacent consonants. In the government programme *Letters and Sounds* (DfES, 2007) it is envisaged that these phases will be covered by the end of Reception. Phase 5 is largely covered in Year 1, where children learn new vowel and consonant digraphs, and also learn that some vowel digraphs have alternative pronunciations (e.g. 'cow', 'blow'), and that some sounds have alternative spellings. To do well on the Phonics Check most of Phase 5 needs to be covered by the end of Year 1 (see Chapter 8). In Phase 6, children learn about prefixes and suffixes, and the phonic rules for adding suffixes (e.g. hope -> hoping, hop -> hopping).

In Reception we found that all ten schools had used a systematic synthetic phonics programme plus graded readers, and eight out of ten had also used decodable readers. All of the children had been taught to sound and blend for reading, but eight of the schools had also taught the children to read high frequency words as sight words, and seven schools had taught the children to read common exception (tricky) words in this way. Furthermore, in eight schools the children had been taught to use picture cues to decode unfamiliar words when reading text, seven schools had encouraged them to use initial letter sounds, and seven schools had encouraged them to use the context. There was evidence therefore of most children being taught to use a sight word approach for reading high frequency and common exception (tricky) words, and to use multiple cues for decoding unfamiliar words in text. In terms of spelling, again there was evidence of mixed methods being used: in seven schools children were taught to segment spoken words for spelling, and six schools reported teaching via the whole word 'look, say, cover, write and check' approach, largely for high frequency and common exception (tricky) words. We have responses from seven of the schools about the pace of teaching: most of the faster learners had progressed to Phase 4 by the end of Reception, and one school had started on Phase 5 work, but the slower learners generally worked on Phase 3 in Reception, with only some covering Phase 4.

From the Year 1 questionnaires we found that nine of the ten schools reported that they had taught the children to read by sounding and blending. However, seven of the schools reported teaching children to use a sight word approach for reading high frequency words, and six schools used the approach with common exception (tricky) words. In eight schools the use of picture cues to decode unfamiliar words in text was used, in seven schools the children were encouraged to use initial letter sounds, and in eight schools they were encouraged to use context cues. There was therefore evidence again that the children in most of the schools were being taught to read high frequency and common exception (tricky) words by sight, and to use multiple cues to decode unfamiliar words when reading text. We also asked about spelling, and found that in eight schools the children were encouraged to use segmenting for spelling, but five schools used the 'look, say, cover, write and check' approach for high frequency and common exception (tricky) words. Information was obtained from seven schools on the pace of the phonics teaching: the fastest learning children in all seven schools worked on Phase 5 level work; for the slower learners, in one school they covered Phase 3 work, in three schools they covered Phase 4 work, and in three schools they covered some Phase 5 work. It seems clear that quite a lot of the slowest learning children were not covering the Phase 5 level work needed for the Phonics Check (see Chapter 8). If slower learning children can cope with a faster pace so that they cover Phase 5 level work in Year 1, as we found they did in some of the study schools, then this would benefit them greatly when sitting the Phonics Check.

These findings from our small-scale study are mirrored in a much larger study carried out by the National Foundation for Educational Research (NFER) for the Department for Education (Walker *et al.*, 2013, p23). It was found that there is generally some confusion about the teaching of systematic synthetic phonics. 53% of teachers in the study agreed with the statement that phonics should be taught first and fast, however 85% of those respondents also agreed with the contradictory statement that a variety of different methods should be used to teach children to decode words. In addition, a further 26% of the sample agreed with the statement that phonics should be taught directly alongside other cueing strategies, and 5% said that phonics is always integrated as one of a range of cueing strategies.

Overview of *Letters and Sounds*

The NFER study (Walker *et al.*, 2013) found that around half the schools in England were still using the government synthetic phonics scheme *Letters and Sounds* (DfES, 2007), which replaced the previous programme *Progression in Phonics* (DfEE, 1999) and its supplement *Playing with Sounds* (DfES, 2004). Although this programme is fully aligned with the National Curriculum, we now know that in actual teaching practice children are being taught to read words by sight and to use multiple cues when reading text, as well as using the synthetic phonics approach.

Letters and Sounds adopts the Simple View of Reading (see Chapter 3), which identifies two processes in reading: recognising words and comprehending text. The 'Notes of Guidance' section of *Letters and Sounds* states that in the early days of learning to read children need to learn how to recognise printed words. Once they have acquired some decoding skill, children can make sense of simple written sentences using the same processes that they use to understand spoken language. When children can recognise and spell words with ease, they will be able to concentrate on understanding what they read and produce good written work. The role of synthetic phonics teaching, therefore, is to establish the children's word recognition and spelling skills early on in their schooling, as a basis for developing good reading comprehension and writing skills.

We can now look in detail at the teaching method outlined in *Letters and Sounds*.

Learning about letters

According to *Letters and Sounds* children should:

- learn to distinguish letter shapes from other letter shapes;
- learn to associate letter shapes with sounds, and vice versa;
- learn letter formation;
- learn to associate letter shapes with names, and vice versa.

In synthetic phonics programmes, letters and their sounds (or more accurately, grapheme-to-phoneme correspondences) are taught in an incremental sequence. In *Letters and Sounds*, as each new grapheme is taught, children blend for reading and segment for spelling using the new and the previously taught graphemes.

Letters and Sounds gives a lot of guidance on how to teach the letters; the key idea here is that letter learning should be multi-sensory. This means that letter formation should be taught right from the start; as children learn a letter sound, they also learn to form it in the air, and then on a whiteboard or piece of paper. Learning the visual appearance, the writing movement, and the sound of a letter all at the same time helps them to consolidate it in memory. *Letters and Sounds* also recommends children use magnetic boards in pairs, to reinforce work done by the teacher on a large magnetic board. This sort of multi-sensory approach is very effective, and is the approach we used in Clackmannanshire. Some synthetic phonics schemes also use mnemonics to help children learn the letter sounds. These mnemonics might involve associating a letter with a character whose name starts with that sound, e.g. the letter 'j' might be represented by a character called Jim. Other approaches involve hand actions and distinctive sounds. The 'Notes of Guidance' (pp14 and 15) says that mnemonics have proved beneficial in helping children remember letters. However, it says that teachers should take care that children understand that the mnemonic and multi-sensory activities (such as drawing, painting, making models, and becoming involved in stories) carried out for reinforcing letter learning are not an end in themselves. Children need to stay focussed on the role of letters in reading and spelling words.

Another issue covered by the 'Notes of Guidance' (p15) is when to introduce letter names: it points out that they will be needed by the start of Phase 3. You will find that it is difficult to teach about vowel digraphs without using letter names. It is problematical to say (using the letter sounds) that /a/ and /i/ together sound as /ai/ as in 'bait'. Early on in our studies, we first introduced letter names when we got to the point of teaching vowel and consonant digraphs (e.g. 'ai', 'th'). However, synthetic phonics is taught so rapidly that we soon realised that it makes sense to teach the letter names before the programme starts. Children often know an alphabet song from the nursery, so it is easy to use the song they already know whilst showing them a visual representation of the letters.

Teaching of high frequency and common exception (tricky) words

In many classes high frequency and common exception words are taught by sight, as we saw above, but this is not the method advocated in *Letters and Sounds*. This approach is a carryover from earlier practice, but it is not clear that it was ever the intention of the authors of *Progression in Phonics* (DfEE, 1999) that this should happen. On page 7 of the manual it says that 'The high frequency words listed in the back of the Framework are not intended to be taught by rote'.

A sight or rote approach with decodable words is undesirable in a synthetic phonic programme, as the aim of the teaching is for children to recognise words by a mature form of sight-word reading well underpinned by letter–sound information (see Chapter 3 for Ehri's model). On page 15 of 'Notes of Guidance', *Letters and Sounds* says:

> High-frequency words have often been regarded in the past as needing to be taught as 'sight words' – words which need to be recognised as visual wholes without much attention to the grapheme to phoneme correspondences in them, even when those correspondences are straightforward. Research has shown, however, that even when words are recognised apparently at sight, this recognition is most efficient when it is underpinned by grapheme–phoneme knowledge. Even the core of high-frequency words which are not transparently decodable using known grapheme–phoneme correspondences usually contain at least one GPC that is familiar. Rather than approach these words as though they were unique entities, it is advisable to start from what is known and register the 'tricky bit' in the word. Even the word yacht, often considered one of the most irregular of English words, has two of the three phonemes represented with regular graphemes.

This means that any teaching using flash cards, where the children are expected to read words visually, seriously undermines the synthetic phonics method. Furthermore, many of the words which are of high frequency in children's books will rapidly become fully decodable, as the synthetic phonics method is so accelerated. Indeed, according to the Core Position Papers (Primary National Strategy, 2006), Phases 2 and 3 of *Letters and Sounds* should take only a maximum of 18 weeks to complete. Thus children will be able to decode many high frequency words via a phonics approach soon after starting school.

Letters and Sounds: Notes of Guidance (p12) also states that children should not use unreliable strategies when dealing with unfamiliar words, such as looking at pictures, rereading the sentence, saying the first sound and guessing the word. These approaches were commonly used alongside *Progression in Phonics* (DfEE, 1999) and *Playing with Sounds* (DfES, 2004), but these strategies encourage a primitive sight word approach to reading not well underpinned by letter sound information (see Chapter 3). This approach is very undesirable, not the least because individuals with a reading disability often find it very hard to break out of this way of dealing with the printed word (Johnston, 1985).

When should children start to read books?

There is a commonly held belief that synthetic phonics necessarily involves a late start to reading text. *Letters and Sounds* recommends an early start to reading decodable texts, firstly through caption reading and then through sentences. Similarly, in our studies the children read captions as soon as they had learnt three or four letters. For example, after teaching 's', 'a', 't', 'p', the children could read 'a tap', 'Pat at a tap', 'Pat sat at a tap'. As more and more letters were learnt, the children increasingly read fully formed sentences. The children also started using reading scheme books about six weeks after the synthetic phonics programme began. These books were not 'decodable' readers, but the phonics teaching was very effective without this resource; the teachers prepared the children beforehand for any words that were not fully decodable. However, many decodable readers are available now to use alongside synthetic phonics schemes.

Fidelity to programme

Letters and Sounds: Notes of Guidance makes it very clear that once you have selected the synthetic phonics programme you are going to use, you should follow it consistently. This is not a situation in which you can cherry pick the parts that appeal to you, these programmes have a tried and tested sequence that optimally develops children's phonic skills. This is analogous to maths teaching, where sticking to the progression worked out by the programme's authors leads to the most effective learning by the children. Learning to decode the printed word is a similarly technical matter, but there will be plenty of opportunities in the language area of the curriculum for you to show your creativity as a teacher!

A typical synthetic phonics lesson

Letters and Sounds: *Six-phase Teaching Programme* gives a great deal of guidance on what synthetic phonics lessons should include, and how to implement the various elements phase by phase. However, below we show what a typical *Letters and Sounds* synthetic phonics lesson looks like (we will look in detail at how to teach lessons in Phases 2 and 5 in Chapters 6 and 7 respectively).

Introduction: Objectives and criteria for success

Revisit and Review: Quick-fire practice of previously taught graphemes and phonemes

Teach: The new grapheme for the day is introduced, and its sound given

The children search for this new letter in letter fans to develop their visual discrimination

The children learn to read and spell a few common exception (tricky) words by having their attention drawn to the decodable and less decodable parts of the words

Practice: Using the new grapheme together with previously taught ones, the children sound and blend printed words for reading, segment spoken words for spelling, and practise writing the new grapheme

Apply: The children read or write captions and sentences using common exception (tricky) words and words made up from the taught graphemes

Assess: Learning against criteria

Although the *Letters and Sounds* scheme has not been tested experimentally in classes like our programme has, it follows our approach so closely that we are confident that if you follow the procedures it outlines your pupils will make a very good start in learning to read. However, it should be pointed out that *Letters and Sounds* has less revision of the previous day's words used for blending and segmenting than there is in our programme; this benefits all children, especially slower learners. Additionally, the effects of the play-like approach described in *Letters and Sounds* has not been tested experimentally. The caution given in *Letters and Sounds* about the use of mnemonics in letter learning also applies here – it is important to be sure that the children are focussing on the phonic goal of the activity, and not on the play element itself.

The lesson plans for each phase outlined in *Letters and Sounds* (see below) show it to be a highly structured method of teaching, and teachers have produced daily lessons using the suggested letter order and the word banks of regular and common exception (tricky) words. If you are new to teaching, you might find it easier to use a commercial programme that meets the Department for Education's criteria (see Chapter 9 for an outline of two commercial programmes that were approved for matched funding). You should be able to find a programme containing fully detailed daily lesson plans, as well as electronic and photocopiable resources to support those lessons. You will also find that commercial programmes provide formative and summative assessments along the lines recommended in *Letters and Sounds*.

Assessment

In order to teach effectively it is important to know how well the children are doing, and this may not be apparent just through observation. *Letters and Sounds* recommends reliable individual assessment of children's learning as they move through the phases. The skills to be assessed are summarised phase by phase in Appendix 3 of *Letters and Sounds*. In summary, children should be able to:

a) give the phonemes to all or most of the taught graphemes;
b) find those graphemes when given the phonemes;
c) write the letters for the graphemes;
d) blend to read words made up from the taught phonemes;
e) segment a spoken word and make a phonemically plausible attempt to spell it
f) read the taught 'tricky' (common exception) words.

The level of skill required for d), e), and f) in particular increases across the phases. You can read more about how to diagnose the problems of slower learners in Chapter 7, where we describe assessments appropriate to the phases. We also give an example in Chapter 8 of how such assessments were used to plan the learning support programme of a child with special educational needs.

Ability group versus whole class teaching

Letters and Sounds gives no advice on whether children should be taught in small groups according to ability, or on a whole class basis. However, when speaking about assessment it does seem to suggest that children should have complete mastery of what they have been taught before continuing with the programme. In practice, there has been a tendency for schools to teach children in ability groups according to the phonics phases (see below for more details of the phases), with children working in that phase until they have mastered it. This is not necessary, however, because any letter–sound correspondences that are not fully secure in one phase will come up in the subsequent phases, and so the learning of them will continue to be reinforced. In fact, the phases outlined in *Letters and Sounds* are not necessary at all in a synthetic phonics programme. For example, it is proposed for Phase 2 that only the first 19 letters of the alphabet should be taught, using words without adjacent consonants; this severely limits what the children can read at this stage, especially if they do not progress until all of these letter sounds have been learnt. The rest of the alphabet is taught in Phase 3, with some consonant and vowel digraphs, but adjacent consonants are not introduced until Phase 4. In fact, many children are able to read words containing adjacent consonants very early on and do not need to be restricted in this way.

In our study in Clackmannanshire the children were taught on a whole class basis for 16 weeks, and this proved to be very beneficial for the slower learners. They were constantly exposed to new print vocabulary, and to the processes of blending and segmenting, and were able to see what the goals of the programme were. They would not have had these benefits if they had proceeded at a very much slower pace than other groups in the class. The teachers in Clackmannanshire found they were also able to keep the class together for phonics lessons throughout the second year of school.

We recommend, from our experience, that children who are slow to learn the letter sounds, and to blend and segment, do well if they get extra practice in a 'nurture' group at some other time during the day, staying with their classmates for the phonics lessons rather than working through the programme more slowly. This may sound surprising, but the low level of underachievement we found in our study in Clackmannanshire (see Chapter 1) shows that keeping all of the children together in the class programme is very effective. Slowing down the programme for some slower learning children may be setting them up for reading failure; they may never catch up with their classmates, however much extra practice in reading they get.

Letters and Sounds lessons and the Phonics Phases

The *Letters and Sounds* programme is split into six phases. These phases are outlined in *The Primary Framework for Literacy and Mathematics* (Primary National Strategy, 2006). *Letters and Sounds: Notes of Guidance* makes it very clear that the boundaries between the phases are not fixed. Phonics starts in Phase 2. Phase 1 prepares for Phase 2, and has activities designed to develop children's oral blending and segmenting of the sounds in spoken words, as well as speaking and listening skills. However, it is made clear in *Letters and Sounds: Notes of Guidance* that children do not need to complete all seven aspects of the Phase 1 programme before starting Phase 2, and indeed Phase 1 work can run alongside Phase 2 work. This view is supported by our research (see Chapter 1), which showed that children who started with no awareness of phonemes, and an inability to produce even one rhyming word, nevertheless made very good progress with synthetic phonics. This is because the fundamental skills of blending and segmenting are very much easier to teach through the medium of letters and print than through purely oral activities. The visual information from print makes blending and segmenting less abstract and more meaningful. Phonemes in themselves are very abstract and difficult to grasp; as adults we think of them in terms of the letter(s) that represent them, and it is beneficial for children to do that as well.

The phases are a convenient way of showing the progression that children's learning will take.

Phase 1

This work is to be carried out in the Early Years Foundation Stage. It is not part of the phonics programme, but prepares children for phonic work. The activities are designed to get children to listen and to discriminate between sounds. The activities are arranged under seven aspects:

1. General sound discrimination – environmental sounds
2. General sound discrimination – instrumental sounds
3. General sound discrimination – body percussion

4. Rhythm and rhyme
5. Alliteration
6. Voice sounds
7. Oral blending and segmenting

In Appendix 2 we have included a daily programme of lessons that covers Aspect 7: Oral blending and segmenting. However, we do not think it is necessary to carry out such a teaching programme before starting teaching synthetic phonics. Forty percent of our sample in the Clackmannanshire Study got no scores at all on phoneme awareness and rhyme tests when they started school. Furthermore, the children who did the synthetic phonics programme early on developed better phoneme awareness skills than the analytic-phonics taught group that did this additional phoneme awareness training programme (Johnston and Watson, 2004, Experiment 1).

We have found in our research that there are other skills that can usefully be taught before Phase 2 starts, such as the conventions of print, the vocabulary of reading, and learning letter names. Much of this can be done when reading stories with the children. You can discuss:

- the left-to-right and top-to bottom directionality of print;
- that words are made up of letters, and that spaces are used between words;
- the use of lower and upper case letters and punctuation;
- positional words such as page, top, bottom, beginning, end, first, middle, last, right, left;
- you can also teach an Alphabet Song, which the children sing while the letters on the board are pointed out.

Phase 2

The basic lesson plan in *Letters and Sounds* is as follows:

Introduction:	Objectives and criteria for success
Revisit and Review:	Practise previously learned letters
	Practise oral blending and segmentation
Teach:	Teach a new letter
	Teach blending and/or segmentation with letters (weeks 2 and 3)
	Teach one or two 'tricky' words (week 3 onwards)
Practice:	Practise reading and/or spelling words with the new letter
Apply:	Read or write a caption (with the teacher) using one or more high-frequency words and words containing the new letter (week 3 onwards)
Assess:	Learning against criteria

This phase starts in Reception; the duration is intended to be up to six weeks, in which time 19 letters are taught. To start with, children learn about the visual appearance, the sounds, and the formation of the letters s, a, t, p, i, n. Synthetic phonics gets going when four letter sounds have been taught, in the second week of Phase 2. That is, once children have learnt a few consonants and at least one vowel, they can begin sounding and blending for reading, and segmenting for spelling, building on the oral blending and segmenting that they have been carrying out in Phase 1.

Sounding and blending

In blending for reading, the child sees a printed word he or she does not know, converts the letters into sounds from left to right, and then blends these sounds together to find out what the word is. An example of sounding and blending follows.

> The child sees the word 'pat', but cannot instantly recognise it. However, she knows the letter sounds for 'p', 'a' and 't'. She says these sounds from left to right, and then blends them together to find out that the word is 'pat'.
>
> **Here is a made-up word – 'pralimtoren'. Using the letter sounds see what you come up with as you blend the sounds from left to right. Given your level of reading skill you may not have needed to do this letter by letter.**

Segmenting for spelling

In segmenting for spelling the child hears the word, breaks it down into its constituent sounds, and then maps these sounds on to the letters. Segmenting for spelling is not traditionally part of synthetic phonics, but it is a very helpful development of the method as it promotes phonemic awareness and a systematic approach to spelling. An example of segmenting for spelling follows.

> The child hears the word 'sat'. She says the word, works out the first sound is /s/, and pulls down the letter 's' on her magnetic board. She says the word again, and hears that the middle sound is /a/, and pulls down the letter 'a'. Then she says the word again, and hears that the final sound is /t/. She pulls down the letter 't'.
>
> She now has 's a t' on her board. She blends these letter sounds together to check she has the letters in the right order.

Letter formation

Children learn to write the letters at the same time as learning the sounds in *Letters and Sounds*, forming them in the air, on a whiteboard, and on paper using pencils. However, they can do their *spelling* using magnetic letters on a board until they have the physical co-ordination necessary for writing the letters with a pencil.

Summary of Phase 2

The key idea here is that children understand that blending and segmenting are reversible processes. Using sounding and blending for reading, and segmenting for spelling, children soon read and spell simple VC and CVC words, such as 'at', 'sat' and 'pat'. The children read and spell more and more new words as each letter sound is taught. They will learn that some words are 'tricky' (i.e. are common exception words), either because they have irregular spellings, or because they are not yet decodable, but these will not be taught purely as sight words. They will also learn to read some two-syllable words.

Phase 3

The basic lesson plan in *Letters and Sounds* is as follows:

Introduction:	Objectives and criteria for success
Revisit and Review:	Practise previously learned letters or graphemes
Teach:	Teach new graphemes
	Teach one or two tricky words
Practice:	Practise blending and reading words with a new GPC (i.e.
	grapheme to phoneme correspondence)
	Practise segmenting and spelling words with a new GPC
Apply:	Read or write a caption or a sentence using one or more tricky words and words containing the graphemes
Assess:	Learning against criteria

This phase is intended to last for up to 12 weeks. A major difference from Phase 2 is that the children now learn that some sounds in our language are spelt by more than one letter, e.g. the consonant digraph 'sh' as in 'shop', the vowel digraph 'oa' as in 'boat'. However, children are *not* taught that the 'oa' sound can also be spelt as 'note'; this introduction to the variability of spelling in English comes in Phase 5. Altogether, 25 new graphemes are taught in this phase, made up of the remaining letters of the alphabet, and some vowel and consonant digraphs. By the end of this phase the children will have learnt to read and spell using one grapheme for each of 43 phonemes. These phonemes are shown in a table on page 11 of *Letters and Sounds: Notes of Guidance*. Many of the consonant phonemes are shown in the initial position of words, for ease of presentation for teachers. However, letter sounds are taught all through the word in synthetic phonics, so the example of /m/ – 'map' could easily have been shown as /m/ – 'ham'.

Phase 4

The basic lesson plan in *Letters and Sounds* is as follows:

Introduction:	Objectives and criteria for success
Revisit and Review:	Practise previously learned graphemes
Teach:	Teach blending and segmentation of adjacent consonants
	Teach some tricky words
Practice:	Practise blending and reading words with adjacent consonants
	Practise segmention and spelling words with adjacent consonants
Apply:	Read or write sentences using one or more high-frequency words and words containing adjacent consonants
Assess:	Learning against criteria

The typical duration of this phase is four to six weeks. Here children learn about adjacent consonants, e.g. 'slip', 'camp'. Most synthetic phonics schemes introduce this much earlier, generally once all the single letter sounds have been taught. This is because reading words with adjacent consonants comes very easily to children who can sound and blend. Indeed, *Letters and Sounds: Notes of Guidance* specifically points out that many children will be capable of taking this step much earlier than Phase 4. In our study in Clackmannanshire, we successfully taught the reading and spelling of words with adjacent consonants from just a few weeks into the programme. The late introduction of adjacent consonants in *Letters and Sounds* is probably a carry over from analytic phonics, where such items were taught in word families, e.g. 'slip', 'slot'. However, it should be stressed that children should not be taught families of words in this way. Our studies have shown that this approach can impede the progress of slower learning children. It is expected that Phase 4 teaching will be completed before the end of Reception; Phases 2 to 4 should take a maximum of 24 weeks teaching to complete. This completes the learning needed for section 1 of the Phonics Check (see Chapter 8).

Phase 5

The basic lesson plan in *Letters and Sounds* is as follows:

Introduction:	Objectives and criteria for success
Revisit and Review:	Practise previously learned graphemes
	Practise blending and segmentation
Teach:	Teach new graphemes
	Teach tricky words
Practice:	Practise blending and reading words with the new GPC (i.e.
	grapheme to phoneme correspondence)
	Practise segmenting and spelling words with the new GPC
Apply:	Read or write a sentence using one or more high-frequency words and words containing the new graphemes
Assess:	Learning against criteria

Phase 5 extends through Year 1, and much of this level of learning is covered in Section 2 of the Phonics Check (see Chapter 8). Up to this point, the children have generally learnt one grapheme for each of the sounds in spoken English. They will have read some words with more than one syllable, some words with vowel and consonant digraphs, and also words with adjacent consonants. They now learn more new digraphs, mainly vowel digraphs. At this point they will start to learn that some spellings have alternative pronunciations, e.g. 'cow', 'blow', and some sounds have alternative spellings, e.g. 'jump', 'hedge'. There are some phonic rules to guide children here, for example in how to spell the /j/ sound at the end of a word, but of necessity some word-specific spellings will need to be learnt.

Phase 6

Letters and Sounds does not suggest a lesson plan for this phase, but we have found it possible to use the lesson plan we outlined in Table 4.1. This phase begins in, and continues throughout, Year 2. By now most children should be able to recognise a large number of words without sounding and blending them; that is, they should show fluency and automaticity in reading familiar words. However, they will still need to sound and blend unfamiliar words. A lot of the teaching in this phase revolves around spelling, as these skills are harder to develop than reading, but this has pay-offs for reading. When we add prefixes, e.g. '<u>re</u>turn' and suffixes, e.g. 'sitt<u>ing</u>', we are adding grammatical morphemes to root morphemes (such as 'turn' and 'sit') that children know very well. Children's reading will become more fluent if they recognise these familiar chunks, and so sound and blend them at the syllable level, e.g. re/place. This awareness of the grammatical morphemes will develop as you teach children the spelling rules for adding them on to base words. For example, where there is a long vowel sound, e.g. 'hope', the 'e' that lengthened the vowel sound is taken off, and –ing is added, forming 'hoping'. However, words with short vowel sounds, e.g. 'hop', have their last letter doubled up, e.g. 'hopping'. Discrete phonics teaching continues, with children learning about the less common grapheme to phoneme correspondences, and also about phonic irregularities. Some spellings are word specific and just have to be learnt; if you are in any doubt about the variability of English vowel spelling, have a look at these words: due/zoo/blew/you!

A SUMMARY OF **KEY POINTS**

➤ According to the National Curriculum, sounding and blending is the primary means by which children should attempt to read all unfamiliar words, including high frequency and common exception (tricky) words; no words should be taught by sight.

➤ According to the National Curriculum, children should not be taught to guess unfamiliar words from picture cues or context.

➤ According to the National Curriculum, children should learn to segment spoken words for spelling; this includes common exception words, where their attention should be drawn to the grapheme–phoneme correspondences that do not fit with what they have been taught so far.

➤ You can assess your pupils' learning from time to time to see if they have learnt the grapheme–phoneme associations you have taught, and see if they can use them to sound and blend for reading and segment for spelling.

➤ We recommend that slower learners stay in the class programme, but do catch-up activities at other times during the day.

➤ *Letters and Sounds* advises that fidelity to the programme you have selected is essential, so it is not advisable to cherry pick from it.

➤ *Letters and Sounds* has six phases, of which Phases 2 to 6 cover phonics. As the children progress through the phonics phases, children learn to read and spell:

- simple CVC words, like 'sat';
- words with consonant and vowel digraphs, like '<u>sh</u>op', 'c<u>oa</u>t';
- words with adjacent consonants, like '<u>sl</u>ip', 'ca<u>mp</u>';
- vowel digraphs with variable pronunciations, like 'c<u>ow</u>', 'bl<u>ow</u>';
- consonants and vowels with alternative spellings, e.g. 'jump', 'he<u>dge</u>';
- words with prefixes and suffixes, e.g. '<u>re</u>turn', 'sit<u>ting</u>';
- rules for adding suffixes, like 'hope'->'hoping', 'hop'->'hopping'.

REFERENCES REFERENCES **REFERENCES** REFERENCES REFERENCES REFERENCES

DfE (2012) Criteria for assuring high-quality phonic work. London: DfE. http://www.education.gov.uk/schools/teachingandlearning/pedagogy/phonics/a0010240/criteria-for-assuring-high-quality-phonic-work (retrieved 17 March 2014).

DfE (2013) *The National Curriculum in England*. London: DfE. https://www.gov.uk/government/publications/national-curriculum-in-england-primary-curriculum (retrieved 20 May 2014).

DfEE (1999) *Progression in Phonics*. London: DfEE. No longer on government website. Available at http://www.amazon.co.uk/National-Literacy-Strategy-Progression-Whole-Class/dp/0193122375/ref=sr_1_1?s=booksandie=UTF8andqid=1394185289andsr=1-1and-keywords=progression+in+phonics

DfES (2004) *Playing with Sounds: A Supplement to Progression Phonics*. London: DfES. No longer on government website. Available at http://www.amazon.co.uk/Playing-With-Sounds-Supplement-Progression/dp/B001PDS7U6

DfES (2007) *Letters and Sounds*. London: DfES. https://www.gov.uk/government/publications/letters-and-sounds (retrieved 27 August 2014).

Johnston, P.H. (1985) Understanding Reading Disability: A Case Study Approach. *Harvard Educational Review*, 55, 153–77.

Johnston, R.S., Walker, J., Howatson, K. and Stockburn, A. (in preparation) What kinds of difficulties do slower learners experience in the Phonics Check?

Johnston, R.S. and Watson, J. (2004) Accelerating the development of reading, spelling and phonemic awareness. *Reading and Writing*, 17(4), 327–57.

Primary National Strategy (2006) *The Primary Framework for Literacy and Mathematics: Guidance for practitioners and teachers on progression and pace in the teaching of phonics (Annex B Outline of Progression)*. London: DfES. http://www.standards.dfes.gov.uk/primary/features/primary/pri_fwk_corepapers/ (retrieved 27 August 2014).

Walker, M., Bartlett, S., Betts, H., Sainsbury, M. and Meta, P. (2013) *Evaluation of the phonics screening check*. NFER research report, May. London: DfE. https://www.gov.uk/government/uploads/system/uploads/attachment_data/file/198994/DFE-RR286A.pdf (retrieved 17 March 2014).

5
How do I start to teach synthetic phonics?

Learning objectives

In this chapter, you will learn how to:

- start to teach the basic skills for synthetic phonics;
- help your children to acquire alphabet knowledge;
- introduce children to letter sounds and letter formation;
- blend (synthesise) letter sounds together to read words;
- break up (segment) the sounds in words to spell;
- teach your children the procedures for blending and segmenting;
- evaluate your children's learning regularly for formative/diagnostic assessment purposes;
- teach the reading and spelling of high frequency and common exception (tricky) words by a synthetic phonics approach.

TEACHERS' STANDARDS

3. Demonstrate good subject and curriculum knowledge
4. Plan and teach well structured lessons
5. Adapt teaching to respond to the strengths and needs of all pupils
6. Make accurate and productive use of assessment

How do I start to teach synthetic phonics?

In addressing this question, we will describe the planning and philosophy underlying the use of systematic synthetic phonics (which includes segmenting words for spelling). It is a balanced approach integrating reading, writing, spelling and phonemic awareness, coupled with relevant language activities (Watson and Johnston, 2000). In this chapter we will show you how to do a lesson that follows the recommendations made in *Letters and Sounds* (DfES, 2007), and the statutory requirements in the National Curriculum (DfE, 2013). Where relevant, compliance with recommendations in the Rose Review (2006) will be indicated.

Our writing system is alphabetic and the Rose Review (2006) points out that 'all beginner readers have to come to terms with the alphabetic principles if they are to learn to read and write' (para. 34). The letters of the alphabet (graphemes) represent the speech sounds of the language (phonemes) and children need to learn that letters must be connected to their sounds in order to pronounce unfamiliar printed words (Watson and Johnston, 2000).

In this and the following chapter, we will explain not only how to develop your children's knowledge of letter–sound correspondences but also how they learn to use this knowledge to sound and blend for reading and to segment for spelling. We will describe how to teach the various elements of a synthetic phonics programme in this chapter, and in Chapter 6 we will explain how to integrate all of these basic elements into a specific lesson.

Teaching the alphabet – letter names, letter sounds and letter formation

In our research in schools (Watson, 1998), we found that the teaching of letter sounds preceded the teaching of letter names. In fact, in many cases letter names were not taught until Year 1 (Primary 2). For many years it had been thought that it was confusing for children to learn both together (Rose Review, 2006). However, as letters of the alphabet are known by their letter names (and in certain instances the sound of a vowel digraph, e.g. 'ai' is the letter name /ai/), it is logical to teach both letter names and letter sounds together. The Rose Review (Rose, 2006) proposes that it is 'sensible to teach both names and sounds of letters' (para. 81). The pronunciations of many of the letter names actually provide a clue to the letter sounds (see Table 5.1).

Table 5.1 Letters where the names give clues to the sounds of the letter

name	sound	name	sound
bee	/b/	eff	/f/
dee	/d/	ell	/l/
jay	/j/	em	/m/
kay	/k/	en	/n/
pea	/p/	ar	/r/
tea	/t/	ess	/s/
vee	/v/	ex	/x/
zed	/z/		

Letter names taught via alphabet song

In our studies, the letters of the alphabet were initially taught through an alphabet song where the children learnt to associate the letter names with upper and lower case magnetic letters in alphabetic order (Watson and Johnston, 2000). Figure 5.1 sets out the procedure for helping children acquire such alphabet knowledge. The resources needed are as follows:

- a CD player and CD accompaniment for the alphabet song being used;
- a magnetic teaching board/wedge;
- lower and upper case magnetic letters of the alphabet.

The music for 'Twinkle, Twinkle, Little Star' fits well with the words of the alphabet song shown below. The children learn to sing the letter names while the appropriate letters on the magnetic alphabet array are simultaneously pointed out. If the accompaniment is transferred to a CD, that will leave you free for teaching the children. To fit in with

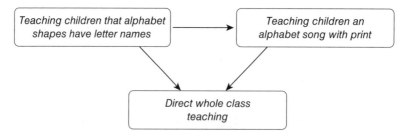

Figure 5.1 Helping children to acquire alphabet knowledge

the music, there is a short introductory section ('Come and listen, listen to me etc', see below). It is also useful to have a short musical introduction on your CD to serve as a signal to the children that the alphabet activity is about to begin.

Words for 'Twinkle Twinkle Little Star'		Words for the alphabet song
Twinkle, twinkle little star	→	Come and listen, listen to me
How I wonder what you are	→	Listen to my a b c
Up above the world so high	→	a b c d e f g
Like a diamond in the sky	→	h i j k lmn o p
Twinkle, twinkle little star	→	q r s t u v
How I wonder what you are	→	w… x y and z

Teaching procedure with the whole class

To teach the alphabet song, match the words and syllables of the letter names to the rhythm of the song. Model the singing, pointing to the letters and encouraging the children to join in. Concentrate on one section at a time and gradually the children will be confident and keen to take part in the singing.

The children can practise the alphabet song daily, taking turns to point to the lower case letters, and then the upper case letters, while singing the letter names. In the electronic version of *Phonics Bug* (Watson and Johnston, 2010), which comes from the programme we used in Clackmannanshire, both the lower case and upper case alphabets are available and the letters are automatically highlighted as the accompaniment is played. The accompaniment can also be clicked off for the children to sing by themselves. We include capital letters because they:

a) provide a way of reinforcing the knowledge that the letter names refer to both lower and upper case letters;

b) reinforce the fact that when the children come to learn the letter sounds, they also share the same sound (Watson and Johnston, 2000); and

c) accelerate the teaching of a sentence. As children know their names start with a capital letter it is only one step further to demonstrate how a capital letter is needed to start a sentence and finish it with a full stop, or indeed an exclamation mark or a question mark.

Introducing letter sounds and letter formation

We found that the children learnt the alphabet well using the teaching sequence of letter shapes, followed by letter names and finally letter sounds.

Before the children can start a synthetic phonics programme, four letter sounds need to be taught in isolation, one at a time (Watson and Johnston, 2000). How each of these letter sounds is taught is described below. When we put a letter in quotation marks, we are indicating the letter name, i.e. 's'. When we put the letter between forward slashes, we are indicating the letter sound, i.e. /s/. Procedures for teaching /s/ on the first day are initially described in detail, and the same procedures are repeated on the following three days for the sounds /a/ /t/ and /p/ (that is, three consonants and one vowel). The sequence for teaching these sounds, which are the first four letters in *Letters and Sounds* (DfES, 2007), is displayed in Figure 5.2.

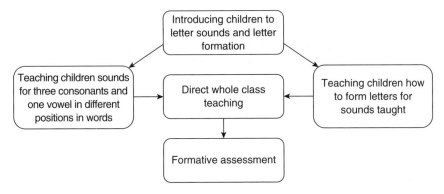

Figure 5.2 Teaching the initial small cluster of sounds together with letter formation

The first four letters in *Letters and Sounds* are s, a, t and p. Table 5.2 illustrates how to teach children the sound and letter formation for the first letter 's' and the required resources.

Note the reversibility aspect of what we want the children to be able to do. Children can

- find the correct letter when given the sound in letter sequences and words;
- say the correct sound when shown the letter – in magnetic form, in print and written form;
- form the letter correctly using a procedural description from the teacher;
- tell the teacher how to write the letter on the board.

Table 5.2 Teaching children the sound and letter formation procedure for 's'.

What we want the children to be able to do	The resources which will be needed
Say the letter name you point out – 's' **Say** 's' sounds /s/. Repeat this 's' sounds /s/ **Point out** the letter which sounds /s/ **Say** the sound for the printed letter – /s/ /s/ /s/ **Say** the sound for the letter written on the board	Magnetic alphabet for the teacher to point out the letter **s** Magnetic alphabet for children to point out **s** Card with the letter **s** in print **s** written on the board
Find the letter for the /s/ sound in letter sequences or words **Say** letter position, i.e. at the beginning, in the middle or at the end of each word	Four cards for letters **z e s x** (If following *Letters and Sounds*, a fan with the letters **s a t p i n**) Four cards for words **pants Stan past spins**
Form the letter 's' following the description given by the teacher **Tell** the teacher how to write the letter 's' on the board	Magnetic letters for **s**, whiteboards and black felt pens Tray with damp sand. Paper and pencil Board and chalk or whiteboard and black felt pen
Talk about what they have learnt	The above lesson plan as an aide memoire

Teaching procedure for Day 1

Display the magnetic alphabet on the teaching magnetic board as below. Sing the alphabet song indicating each letter, lower case then upper case.

A B C D E F G H I J K L M N O P Q R S T U V W X Y Z

a b c d e f g h i j k l m n o p q r s t u v w x y z

▲

Teaching the letter sound: Point to the magnetic letter **s** (see arrow above), asking the children its name, then saying **'s' sounds** /s/. Repeat the sound with the children, then let the children say the sound /s/ on their own. Show the card with **s** printed on it on its own, then ask the children to say the sound. They should say **'s' sounds** /s/. Write the letter **s** on the board asking the children to say the sound again **'s' sounds** /s/.

Searching for the letter 's' in a letter sequence: Replace the letter **s** in the magnetic alphabet array, pull down the letters **z e s x**, and ask the children to point to the letter which sounds /s/. Replace these letters. Repeat the procedure using the pack of cards with the printed individual letters. Display the cards, asking the children to select the card with the letter for the sound /s/. Repeat the procedure, this time writing the four letters on the board and asking the children which one is /s/.

*Searching for letters in letters sequences (*Letters and Sounds*):* An alternative approach is to arrange the letters **s a t p i n** in a fan. The child hears the sound /s/, finds the letter for the sound /s/, leaves it at the top, and slides the other letters out of sight.

Searching for letters in words: Write on the board the four words **pants Stan past spins**. Ask the children to find the letter for the sound /s/ in each of the words, saying whether it is at the beginning, in the middle or at the end of the word. Repeat this visual search showing the words on the cards, the children pointing to the letter for the sound /s/ in each word, saying the position. Return to the words on the board asking the children to draw a circle round the letter for the sound /s/ in each word. (Note that the purpose of these words is for visually identifying the position of the target letter sound in words. Children are not being asked to try to read them.)

Our reason for asking children to identify the position of the target letter sound in words, as well as in a set of letters (as recommended in *Letters and Sounds*, DfES, 2007), is to encourage them to think of the words as an ordered sequence of letters. They need to learn to examine the words in a left-to-right direction and use the correct vocabulary for saying where the letter sound is positioned (Watson and Johnston, 2000).

Teaching children how to form letters for the taught sounds

Using the magnetic letter **s**, demonstrate how to follow round the shape with your finger saying where and how to start, follow the shape round and back and where to stop. Repeat this procedure with the children carrying out the movement from your description with their own magnetic letter **s**, experiencing the shape through using their fingers. Repeat this procedure again with the children joining in with your movement 'jingle'.

Ask the children to place their magnetic **s** letter on the desk beside them and form the letter 's' on top of the desk using their fingers as you and the children describe the movement, where to start, how to continue and where to finish. Now write the letter **s** on the board slowly and deliberately while you and the children simultaneously repeat the movement. Clean the board and invite pairs of children to the board, one to write the letter following the partner's instructions, cleaning the board in between while the children alternate their roles. Finally, ask the children to describe the movement for you to write the letter on the board. The children can practise forming the letter with their fingers a) in damp sand in the tray, b) with a black felt pen on pupil whiteboards and c) with pencil and paper.

Now using your lesson plan as a guide, discuss with the children what they have learnt today:

- they are able to select 's' from the alphabet line;
- they know that the letter 's' sounds /s/;
- they can find it in a group of letters;
- they can find it at the beginning of words, in the middle of words and at the end of words;
- not only can they follow the movement pattern for writing the letter 's', they can also tell someone else how to write it.

Conclude by singing the alphabet song again.

Cleaning the board between the letter formation movements is done to avoid any risk of copying from the board, as the attention would have to be divided between the eye and the hand. The complexities of copying are described in great detail in *The Montessori Principles and Practice* by Culverwell as long ago as 1913. He writes that, instead of relying on the eye to direct the hand, Montessori relies on the motor memory: 'The fingers are trained to remember the movements needed to form the letters' (p120). Learning this movement will help consolidate the letter in memory, together with its visual appearance, its name and its sound.

Teaching procedure for Days 2, 3, and 4
The target letter sound /a/ is taught the next day, and /t/ and /p/ on the following two days, adopting the same procedure as for the letter sound /s/. Before starting to introduce each new target letter sound, review the previous day's teaching. Resources are the same

for each session except for the magnetic letters and letter and word cards for a, t and p (see below).

For learning 'a' sounds /a/, the cards needed are one with **a** in print, cards with **c s w a** in print and cards for words **apple sand zebra banana**.

For learning 't' sounds /t/ the cards needed are one with **t** in print, cards with **f r j t** in print, and cards for words **rabbit actor towel tent**.

For learning 'p' sounds /p/ the cards needed are one with **p** in print, cards with **g o y p** in print and cards for words **stop Penny pat puppet**.

After four days of teaching, the children will be able to identify four letters of the alphabet, know their sounds, and be able to identify the letters in two contexts – in sequences of letters and in words formed from the taught letters. They will also have learnt to form the letters.

The above explicit direct teaching procedures are designed to be presented to the whole class. Practising writing the letter, after the formation procedure has been taught, can be carried out in groups.

Formative/diagnostic assessment

Ongoing formative/diagnostic assessment is an integral part of learning and teaching, and is strongly recommended in *Letters and Sounds* (DfES, 2007). At this pre-programme stage, the teacher will be able to identify from the daily sessions not only the children who are gaining alphabet knowledge and can join in with the alphabet song activity success-fully, but also those children who are proceeding at a slower pace and are not confident at a) singing the alphabet song and/or b) pointing to the letters on the magnetic alphabet simultaneously. In each of the daily sessions, the children have been introduced to one of four basic letter sounds /s/ /a/ /t/ /p/ and the formation of their corresponding letters **s a t p**.

As the teacher displays the target letter in different positions in words, he or she will be able to identify the children who can pronounce the relevant sound correctly. When the children are given the target sound, the teacher can identify the children who are able to recognise the letter in different positions in words, write the related letter or tell a partner or the teacher how to write it.

The record sheet might be as follows:

Score sheet to assess children's knowledge of the letters s a t p

Date:

	Alphabet knowledge				Can give the sound for:				Can write letters for:			
Child's name	Song		With print		's'	'a'	't'	'p'	/s/	/a/	/t/	/p/
	Yes	No	Yes	No								

(See Appendix 3 for full photocopiable sheet.)

REFLECTIVE TASK

REFLECTIVE TASK

Task 2

Having taught the letter sounds and letter formation for three consonants and a vowel, what do you think are the next steps to take?

See the end of the chapter for answers.

Teaching blending for word reading and segmenting for spelling

What are the children going to do with the cluster of letter sounds they have been taught? From the simple words which can be generated using these letters, how can we teach the children to read and spell them? Figure 5.3 sets out a sequence of explicit teaching procedures for just such a purpose, namely blending for word reading and segmenting and blending for spelling. Beginner readers must be taught 'how to blend (synthesise) the sounds to read words and break up (segment) the sounds in words to spell' (Rose, 2006, para. 45).

Teaching blending for word reading

The importance of the blending process in the development of independent reading is highlighted by Feitelson (1988), the skills involved bearing a causal relationship to emerging word recognition skills (Perfetti *et al.*, 1987). The method described by Feitelson (1988) is used in Germany and Austria, which has a strong emphasis on the blending or co-articulating of letters to pronounce words. This is the synthetic phonics approach. Feitelson (1988, pp. 127–133) cites two types of blending procedure:

- the final blending procedure of Richardson *et al.* (1977); and
- the successive blending procedure of Resnick and Beck (1976).

In Resnick and Beck's procedure, the sound of each letter is pronounced and stored in memory. The final blending procedure is only attempted after the sounds of all of the letters have been pronounced and stored in memory e.g. the word **cat**. *Point to 'c', say /k/. Point to 'a', say /a/. Point to 'ca', say /ka/ slowly; repeat, point to 'ca', say /ka/ quickly. Point to 't', say /t/. Point to 'cat', say /kat/ slowly. Point to 'cat' and say /kat/ quickly and smoothly.*

In Richardson *et al.* procedure, the sounds are synthesized successively as the reader goes along e.g. *Point to the beginning of the word 'cat',* say the sounds in sequence *Draw your finger along underneath the word, stretching out the sound, like a piece of elastic, saying /kaaat/ then releasing the stretch, as it were, to say /kaat and /kat/. Point to 'cat' and say /kat/ smoothly.*

The next step, therefore, is to teach blending for word reading. The approach advocated in *Letters and Sounds* (DfES, 2007) fits most closely with Richardson *et al.*'s final blending procedure described above. We partly used this approach in our studies. Pupils sounded out magnetic letters from left-to-right slowly and fluently, stretching out each sound and blending it into its adjacent neighbour without a pause, to produce one single sound from the discrete successive phonemes. Liberman and Liberman (1990) call this co-articulation. This has the advantage of cutting out the 'uh' sound that often follows the pronunciation of letter sounds on their own. Simultaneously, the magnetic letters were pushed together from left-to-right, from the first letter *through* to the last letter to form one complete word as the sounds were co-articulated. When the children do this for themselves, the use of the magnetic letters enables them to physically and visually experience the blending process. (The electronic version of our programme demonstrates the blending process by moving the letters together from left to right).

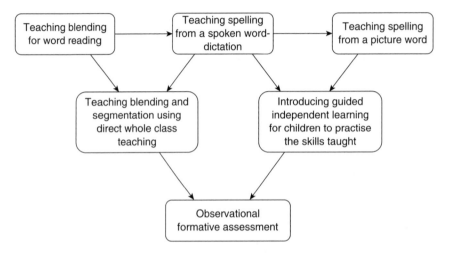

Figure 5.3 Procedures for using initial small cluster of letter sounds taught

Teacher modelling the blending procedure

Target: Children will be able to demonstrate the blending procedure for word reading using magnetic letters.

Resources: Teaching magnetic board, relevant magnetic letters and arrow, word card **pat**

If you have a set of magnetic letters, you may find it helpful to carry out the suggested activities yourself as you read this section.

Place a magnetic arrow (→) on the left-hand side of the magnetic board as a reminder that reading is from left to right. Place the letter **a** on the magnetic board, ask the children to say the sound /a/. Leaving a space after the letter **a** place the letter **t** next to it, **a t**. Ask the children to say the sound /t/. Now demonstrate the blending process. Start to push the **a** towards the **t** while you blend the two sounds /a/ and /t/ together smoothly to sound /at/. Replace the magnetic letters in the alphabet line. Tell the children that when they see a word they don't know, this is the procedure to follow, sounding the letters and blending them together to read that word.

Children trying out the blending procedure (1)

The magnetic arrow (→) can remain on the left-hand side of the magnetic board or be removed at the teacher's discretion. Place the letter **a** on the magnetic board, ask the children to say the sound /a/. Leaving a space after the letter **a** place the letter **s** next to it, **a s**. Ask the children to say the sound /s/. Then ask them to tell you what the next step is before reminding them. Start to push the **a** towards the **s** while they blend the two sounds /a/ and /s/ together smoothly to sound /as/ and read the word.

Children trying out the blending procedure (2)

Place the word **sat** on the magnetic board. *Do not* tell the children what this word is. Ask the children what is the first letter of the word and pull it down: **s**. The children say the sound /s/. Similarly for the second letter of the word, pull it down alongside the first letter, leaving a space as before: **s a**. The children say the middle sound /a/. Bring down the last letter as before, alongside **s a t**, saying the sound /t/. Ask the children to say the first, middle and last sound, i.e. /s/ /a/ /t/, and then start to push the letters together from left to right, while blending the three sounds together smoothly and fluently to sound /sat/ and read **sat**.

Children trying out the blending procedure (3)

Display a printed word for the children to read: **pat**. Point to each letter in succession asking the children to say the sounds /p/ /a/ /t/. Then ask the children to blend the sounds together to read the word, smoothly co-articulating the letter sounds. The children read the word **pat**. (In teaching observations we sometimes see the teachers doing the sounding and blending, with the children listening, but it is most important that the children do this themselves.)

Teaching segmenting for spelling

What do children have to do to spell a word? Children have to:

- be able to break down the spoken word into its letter sounds (phonemes);
- remember the order of the letter sounds; and
- remember the letter shape (the grapheme) for each sound;
- blend the letter sounds together to check that the phonemes in the spoken word map on to the sequence of letters in the printed word.

Procedure for teaching segmenting for word spelling

Target: Children will demonstrate the segmenting procedure for spelling a dictated word

Resources: Teaching magnetic board, relevant magnetic letters and direction arrow

This time the children do not see the target word; they hear it. Say that you want them to help you to spell the word **sat**: 'The puppy **sat** on the mat. Spell the word **sat**'. Ask the children to:

- Repeat the word for spelling **sat**.
- Say the first sound in **sat** (i.e. /s/).
- Find the letter for the sound from the magnetic alphabet and place it on the board **s**.
- Say the second sound in **sat** (i.e. /a/).

- Find the letter from the alphabet and place it next to the first letter on the board **s a**.
- Say the last sound in **sat** (i.e. /t/), find the letter from the alphabet and place it next to the first two letters on the board **s a t**.

Now ask the children to say each sound /s/ /a/ /t/ and blend the sounds together, as for word reading, to make **sat**. Replace the magnetic letters on the alphabet line. Blending the letter sounds together is carried out to check that the sounds in the spoken word map on to the sequence of letters in the printed word.

REFLECTIVE TASK

Task 3

How many words can you make from the letters s a t p?

See the end of the chapter for answers.

Introducing guided independent learning with pupil magnetic boards – skills application

We now want the children to apply the skills they have acquired by working independently, each with a pupil magnetic board or in pairs, sharing a pupil magnetic board and relevant magnetic letters. The pupil magnetic boards are fitted with an alphabet grid and as each letter sound is taught the relevant magnetic letter is placed on the boards. The display below illustrates that at this stage the magnetic letters on the board are **a p s t** together with a magnetic arrow to signify the left-hand side where the children will start to spell the word. The letters not in bold represent the magnetic letters which will only be placed on the alphabet grid after they have been taught.

```
a  b  c  d  e  f  g  h

i  j  k  l  m

n  o  p  q  r  s  t  u

v  w  x  y  z

→
```

Dictated words

Children are asked to spell a word on their magnetic boards. The teacher dictates 'Spell **pats**. Mum **pats** the dog's head. Spell the word **pats**.'

After checking how the children have carried out the task and asking them to read the word produced, namely **pats**, the teacher spells the word on the teaching magnetic board, inviting children to carry out the procedures and replace the letters in the alphabet line as before.

Repeat the procedure for spelling **taps**. 'Our sink has two **taps**. Spell the word **taps**'.

Children replace the letters used on their pupil magnetic boards to their alphabetic position on the grid ready to use again.

Picture words

Instead of a dictated word, children are given/shown a picture e.g. a **tap** and are asked to say the word themselves and spell it on their boards using the same procedures as for dictated words.

Formative/diagnostic assessment

This is ongoing during each session a) through observation of how the children carry out the blending and segmenting procedures during explicit direct teaching and b) through checking how the children carry out each of the tasks given for the guided independent learning.

The heading for a score sheet might be as follows. A code is devised for the recording of blending competence, for example:

1 = unable to blend
2 = cannot produce the correct sound for any letter
3 = can produce the correct sound for one of the letters
4 = can produce the correct sound for all of the letters
5 = can sound and blend successfully

Learning to blend for reading and to segment for spelling takes place as soon as the basic teaching of three consonants and one vowel has been completed. Knowledge of the alphabet can be included again in this score sheet as some of the children who were working at a slower pace earlier on may have made some progress by now.

Score sheet to assess children's ability to sound and blend the letters s a t p

	Blending				Blending				Alphabet				Segmentation		
									Song		Print		Dictation		Picture
Child's name	as	at	sap	sat	tap	taps	pat	pats	Y	N	Y	N	pats	taps	tap

See Appendix 4 for full photocopiable sheet.

REFLECTIVE TASK

Task 4

Recording segmenting for spelling using s a t p

What sort of spelling record of children's progress would you as a teacher find it useful to make before proceeding with the full programme? Devise a record-keeping code for segmentation for spelling from dictation and from a picture.

See the end of the chapter for suggestions for content.

Overview of basic skills acquisition procedures

Figure 5.4 illustrates an overview of the basic procedures adopted for children starting to blend phonemes with graphemes to read words, starting to segment words into sounds and starting to form letters to spell words.

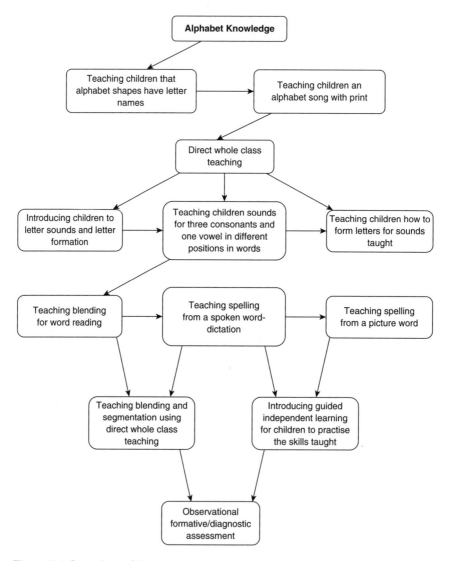

Figure 5.4 Overview of the basic procedures required in the synthetic phonics programme

The teacher's role in implementing the above procedures would be:

- selecting the target(s) to be reached;
- selecting and preparing the relevant resources;

- setting the scene (alphabet song activity with magnetic alphabet and letters);
- modelling the target skill(s) for the children to try out – skills acquisition;
- providing for guided independent practice and learning – skills application;
- evaluating learning through observational formative/diagnostic assessment.

Teaching high frequency and common exception (irregular/tricky) words

We showed in Chapter 4 that in the majority of schools it is still common practice to teach children to recognise high frequency and common exception words by sight, and to spell them by the 'look, say, cover, write and check' approach. *Letters and Sounds* (DfES, 2007) includes a list of 100 high frequency and common exception (tricky) words, but the intention is that they will be taught in such a way that pupils will understand that letter–sound correspondences underpin the reading and spelling of them. This approach has now been made statutory in the National Curriculum (DfE, 2013). The National Curriculum also says children should be taught to read books that are consistent with their developing phonic knowledge and which do not require them to use other strategies to work out the pronunciation of words. This means that children should not be taught to decode the unfamiliar words that they meet in text by looking at picture cues and/or guessing from context; children can work on reading the common exception (tricky) words that are going to come up in a new book before they are given it to read. When you look at the *Letters and Sounds* high frequency word list, split into decodable (Table 5.3) and common exception (tricky) words (Table 5.4), you can see that these words account for a very large proportion of what children read. Indeed, Share (1995) estimates that the 100 most frequent words in children's reading books account for around 50% of what children read. Although the goal of synthetic phonics teaching is the rapid and automatic recognition of words, the phonics method is undermined if half of what children are taught to read is shown on flash cards for sight reading without phonic synthesis.

Table 5.3 High frequency decodable words (DfES, 2007)

a	dad	but	look	time
an	had	put	too	house
as	back	will	went	about
at	and	that	it's	your
if	get	this	from	day
in	big	then	children	made
is	him	them	just	came
it	his	with	help	make
of	not	see	don't	here
off	got	for	old	saw
on	up	now	I'm	very
can	mum	down	by	

Some confusion is caused by the use of the term 'tricky', as some of the regularly spelt words in Table 5.3 have been labelled tricky; this is because at the time at which they are introduced the children have not been taught the relevant phonics, not because they contain unusual spelling–sound correspondences. For example, a reading book may contain words such as 'time', 'made' and 'came' before split digraphs are taught in Phase 5. As only 26 of the items in Table 5.3 are decodable by the end of Phase 2, there is a need for the early use of some of these words so that children can progress to reading captions and books. Other words remain partially decodable because they have irregular spellings; children do also need to learn how to read some of these words early on in order to have a wide reading experience (see Table 5.4). How then should children be taught to tackle words for which they have not yet covered the phonics, and words for which a phonics approach only helps with part of the word?

Table 5.4 Common exception/irregular/'tricky' words (DfES, 2007)

the	me	said	little	Mrs
to	be	have	one	looked
I	was	like	when	called
no	you	so	out	asked
go	they	do	what	could
into	all	some	oh	
he	are	come	there	
she	my	were	people	
we	her	there	Mr	

There is a lot of guidance in Phase 2 of *Letters and Sounds* (DfES, 2007, p64) on the procedure for teaching 'tricky' high frequency words, see Table 5.5. We would like to add that it would also be a good idea to get the children to spell the word at the time they learn to read it, removing the word from view while this is being done. This procedure will also reinforce learning to read the word.

Table 5.5 How to teach 'tricky' high frequency words (DfES, 2007)

1. Explain that there are some words that have one, or sometimes two, tricky letters.
2. Read the caption, pointing to each word, then point to the word to be learned and read it again.
3. Write the word on the whiteboard.
4. Sound-talk the word and repeat putting sound lines and buttons under each phoneme and blending them to read the word.
5. Discuss the tricky bit of the word where the letters do not correspond to the sounds the children know (e.g. in 'go', the last letter does not represent the same sound as the children know in 'dog').
6. Read the word a couple more times and refer to it regularly throughout the day so that by the end of the day the children can read the word straight away without sounding out.

Letters and Sounds also gives advice on how to practise the reading of high frequency words, including 'tricky' ones, once the children have read them phonically (DfES, 2007, p65) (see Table 5.6).

Table 5.6 Practising reading high frequency and 'tricky' words after children have read them via phonics (DfES, 2007)

1. Display a word card.
2. Point to each letter in the word as the children sound-talk the letters (as far as is possible with tricky words) and read the word.
3. Say a sentence using the word, slightly emphasising the word.
4. Repeat 1–3 with each word card.
5. Display each word again, and repeat the procedure more quickly but without giving a sentence.
6. Repeat once more, asking the children to say the word without sounding it out.

It can be seen that children should work with high frequency and common exception (tricky) words in order to understand the role of letter–sound correspondences in pronouncing them, and then move on to learning the rapid recognition of these words without sounding and blending them.

A SUMMARY OF **KEY POINTS**

➢ Children need to learn that letters must be connected to their sounds in order to pronounce unfamiliar printed words.

➢ To help children acquire alphabet knowledge, they are taught an alphabet song with print using lower and upper case magnetic letters.

➢ Using direct whole class teaching, children are taught a small group of letter sounds in different positions in words, together with letter formation. They should be able to identify these letters in sequences of letters and in words formed from the taught letters.

➢ Blending for word reading and segmenting for spelling are explicitly taught using whole class direct teaching, magnetic boards and letters. The children also practise spelling from dictation and from picture words through guided independent learning.

➢ Formative assessment is ongoing through observation of pupil response during explicit direct teaching and monitoring tasks carried out during guided independent learning.

➢ A diagrammatic overview (see Figure 5.4) describes the basic procedures required in the synthetic phonics programme together with the teacher's role in implementing these procedures.

➢ High frequency and common exception/'tricky' words are also taught by a synthetic phonics approach; in the latter case, both the regular and 'tricky' letter–sound correspondences are pointed out, and the sounds are blended.

REFLECTIVE TASK

Task 1 answers

The children can learn:

- that an alphabet has shapes, shapes are letters and letters have names;
- the alphabetic order of the letter names;
- that lower and upper case letters share the same letter name;
- to follow a left-to-right direction of print;
- to start at the beginning;
- to finish at the end.

REFLECTIVE TASK

Task 2 answer

The next steps would be:

- teaching blending for word reading;
- teaching segmenting and blending words for spelling.

REFLECTIVE TASK

Task 3 answer

Words: a, as, at, pat, Pat, pats, sap, sat, tap, taps, past, Papa

REFLECTIVE TASK

Task 4 answer

A segmentation code could take account of what children have to do to spell a word and the columns could be: Yes, Nearly, No.

1 = Can the pupil break down the spoken word into its letter sounds (phonemes)?
2 = Can the pupil remember the order of the letter sounds (phonemes) in the word?
3 = Can the pupil remember the letter shape (grapheme) for each sound?
4 = Can the pupil blend the letter sounds together to check that the sounds (phonemes) in the spoken word map on to the sequence of letters in the printed word?

REFERENCES REFERENCES **REFERENCES** REFERENCES REFERENCES REFERENCES

Culverwell, E.P. (1913) *The Montessori Principles and Practice*. London: Bell & Sons Ltd.

DfE (2013) *The National Curriculum in England*. London: DfE. https://www.gov.uk/government/publications/national-curriculum-in-england-framework-for-key-stages-1-to-4 (retrieved 17 March 2014).

DfES (2007) *Letters and Sounds*. London: DfES. https://www.gov.uk/government/publications/letters-and-sounds (retrieved 27 August 2014).

Feitelson, D. (1988) *Facts and Fads in Beginning Reading. A Cross-Language Perspective*. Norwood NJ: Ablex.

Liberman, I.Y. and Liberman, A.M. (1990) Whole language vs. Code Emphasis. Underlying Assumptions and Their Implications for Reading Instruction. *Annals of Dyslexia*, 40(1), 51–76.

Perfetti, C.A., Beck I., Bell, L. and Hughes C. (1987) Phonemic knowledge and learning to read are reciprocal. A longitudinal study of first grade children. *Merrill-Palmer Quarterly*, 33, 283–319.

Resnick, L.B. and Beck, I.L. (1976) Designing instruction in reading. Interaction of theory and practice. In J.T. Guthrie (Ed.) *Aspects of Reading Acquisition*. Baltimore, MD: John Hopkins University Press. Cited in Feitelson, D. (1988) *Facts and Fads in Beginning Reading. A Cross-Language Perspective*. Norwood, NJ: Ablex. pp130–33.

Richardson, E., Di Benedetto, B. and Bradley, C.M. (1977) The relationship of sound blending to reading achievement. *Review of Educational Research*, 47, 319–34. Cited in Feitelson, D. (1988) *Facts and Fads in Beginning Reading. A Cross-Language Perspective*. Norwood, NJ: Ablex. pp127–30.

Rose, J. (2006) *Independent review of the teaching of early reading: Final Report*. Nottingham: DfES. http://webarchive.nationalarchives.gov.uk/20100408085953/http://standards.dcsf.gov.uk/phonics/rosereview/ (retrieved 27 August 2014).

Share, D. (1995) Phonological recoding and self-teaching: sine qua non of reading acquisition. *Cognition*, 55(2), 182–4.

Watson, J.E. (1998) An investigation of the effects of phonics teaching on children's progress in reading and spelling. PhD thesis. University of St Andrews.

Watson, J.E. and Johnston, R.S. (2000) *Accelerating Reading and Spelling with Synthetic Phonics: A Guide to the Teaching Method*. Edinburgh: Scottish Executive Education Department.

Watson, J.E and Johnston, R.S. (2010) *Phonics Bug*. Harlow: Pearson.

6
Teaching a synthetic phonics lesson in Phase 2 of *Letters and Sounds*

Learning objectives

In this chapter, you will learn how to:

- follow a sample lesson format for teaching a Phase 2 synthetic phonics lesson;
- share targets and success criteria with your children;
- plan quick-fire revision of previously taught sounds, and of words used for reading and spelling the day before;
- teach the new letter sound and how to use it for word reading, spelling and letter formation;
- dictate words for spelling using a word-sentence-word procedure;
- introduce common exception (tricky) words, captions and sentences for reading and spelling;
- evaluate your children's learning regularly for formative/diagnostic assessment purposes;
- analyse decodable readers for fit with progress in letter sound learning, to maximise learning potential.

TEACHERS' STANDARDS

3. Demonstrate good subject and curriculum knowledge
4. Plan and teach well structured lessons
5. Adapt teaching to respond to the strengths and needs of all pupils
6. Make accurate and productive use of assessment

Teaching a synthetic phonics lesson

In this chapter, we will explain how to integrate all the basic elements described in Chapter 5 into one sample lesson format. We will provide an example of this lesson format showing how to teach the letter sound /d/, and how to blend for reading and segment for spelling using this and previously taught letters. In Chapter 7 we will show how to teach the vowel digraph sound /oy/ and how to blend and segment letters and syllables for reading and spelling using the same lesson format. Both sample lessons follow the order of letter sound teaching recommended in *Letters and Sounds* (DfES, 2007) for the Foundation Stage (Primary 1 in Scotland) and Key Stage 1 (Primaries 2 and 3 in Scotland). The single consonant 'd' from Phase 2, and the vowel digraph 'oy' from Phase 5, have been chosen to demonstrate that the programme can be 'followed consistently and carefully, each day, reinforcing and building on previous learning to secure children's progress' (Rose, 2006, para. 56).

Lesson format

Having taught the basic procedures adopted throughout the programme (see Chapter 5), the children are now ready to start doing synthetic phonics lessons. Figure 6.1 shows the teaching sequence which is used to deliver the programme for

a) whole class explicit direct teaching – skills acquisition;
b) children in groups at their tables – practising the skills acquired;
c) children in groups at their tables – application of skills acquired.

Opportunities for skills development outside the lesson format will be described below in the section 'Variations in lesson format and integration with text reading', p.81.

Introduction

1   **Sharing daily targets with the children**

⇓

2   **Revision of previous day's learning**

⇓

3   **Teaching new letter sound**

⇓

4   **Practising skills acquired**

⇓

5   **Apply skills acquired**

⇓

6   **Learning outcomes with the pupils**

⇓

7   **Ongoing formative assessment**

Figure 6.1 Lesson format – sequence for teaching a synthetic phonics lesson

1 Introduction to lesson to teach letter sound /d/

We are going to show a sample lesson based on the procedures outlined in *Letters and Sounds* (DfES, 2007), but fleshed out with our own experience of implementing a successful synthetic phonics programme. In *Phonics Bug* (Watson and Johnston, 2010), which is based on the programme we used in Clackmannanshire, we used:

1. the alphabet song (with print) to signify for the children the start of the session and to help children consolidate their alphabet knowledge;
2. targets for the session to share with the children, talking through what they already knew and what they were now going to learn;
3. the daily lesson plan to provide a structured guide to sharing the target outcomes for the day. The children need to know the criteria for success. Table 6.1 shows a structured format you can use to prompt you for the sequence of activities in the lesson. It can also be used for making notes during the learning outcomes plenary session.

Table 6.1 Structured guide for target sharing

Focus of discussion	Criteria for success	Learning outcomes
Revision **m**	Say the letter and the sound Read four words Spell four words	
Lesson new letter **d**	Say the letter and the sound Find the letter in words, say if it is at the beginning/middle/end/ of the word	
Words with **d**	Read four words Spell four words Write **d**	
Magnetic boards	**d** added to alphabet grid Spell word from teacher Spell two picture words	
a is both a letter and a word captions	Read captions Spell captions with teacher	

At this early stage in the programme, a chart showing a brief outline of the day's lesson can be displayed in a prominent place for the children to refer to. It might look something like Figure 6.2. The second column is meant for the pupils; we have included the first column as an explanation for you.

Today's lesson

alphabet song	♫ ♫
revision	↻ m
lesson	☎ **'d'** **/d/**
find	♋ •--- --•-- ---•
words reading spelling writing	**blend and read** **segment and spell** ✎ **d**
a b c d e f g h i j k l **m n** o **p** q **r s t** u v w x yz	**spell with magnetic letters**
'tricky' words, captions and sentences	**read and spell**
learning outcomes	☺ ☹
alphabet song	♫ ♫

Figure 6.2 Today's lesson

It is economical to design a chart that would only need the revision letter and the new letter changed each day, remembering to change the target letter each day to **bold** print, with the alphabet letters replicating the pupils' magnetic boards. The symbol ↻ signifies returning to the lesson for the day before. The sound of the target letter is represented by the ☎ symbol, while the symbol that looks like two eyes 👓 indicates visually searching for the letter in the words. The dashes ---- represent the letters in a word, and dashes with the bullet point (----•) show where the letter **d** is situated. The pupils have to find **d** and say whether it is at the beginning, middle or end of the word. The symbol 👥 has been used to indicate children working in pairs on the magnetic boards. The happy and sad symbols ☺☹ indicate the Learning Outcomes section, where the children assess how well they have learnt the lesson. While it is hoped most of the children will feel they have been successful, some may want more help.

BEEFECIIΛE IΛ2K

REFLECTIVE TASK

Task 1

Design your own chart suitable for use by your pupils so that they know how the day's lesson will proceed.

2 Revision

Quickfire revision of:

- The most recent letter–sound correspondences taught before **d**, namely **i n m**. Display letter cards one at a time – children pronounce the relevant sounds and the teacher pronounces each sound and children find the correct letter card.
- Sound-talk for the children to practise oral blending and segmentation, e.g. D-a-d is s-a-d. P-a-m sat on the m-a-t. Can you s-i-t on a chair? Suggested words for children to practise sound-talk themselves: pin, doll, train.
- Word reading – display the previous day's spelling words, e.g. 'Tim', 'man', 'mat', 'map'. Ask the children to read them (if they can), or sound, blend and read them.
- Spelling words – pronounce each of the previous day's reading words, e.g. 'Sam', 'am', 'mats', 'Pam' and ask the children to spell them by telling you how to write each letter. (Not only is this quicker than actually asking the children to come out and select magnetic letters or write the letters to spell the words, but also the purpose of telling the teacher how to write them is to see if the children can remember the procedural movement.)

3 Teaching new letter sound, using it for word reading, spelling and letter formation

As described in Chapter 5, introduce the new letter sound in magnetic and print forms. Using direct whole class teaching, and the teacher's magnetic board and letters:

- Model saying **'d' [letter name] sounds /d/**, with the children repeating 'd' sounds /d/.
- Find the position in words (remember – a visual search, not reading!). Display the words **stand damp add Adam**. Ask children to find the letter for /d/ in each word and circle the letter, saying whether it is at the beginning, middle or end of each word. Alternatively, if following *Letters and Sounds* (DfES, 2007), use letter fans.
- Read the words **and dip did dim**. Children *see* the magnetic word/printed word, e.g. **dip**, but it is not pronounced for them. The children sound each letter /d/ /i/ /p/ in turn, then they blend the separate sounds together while the teacher or a child pushes the magnetic letters together to form the word. When the word

is in print, the children draw their fingers along the word as they blend the sounds together. (Our electronic programme, *Phonics Bug* (Watson and Johnston, 2010), carries out the blending process on the electronic whiteboard by pushing the letters together to form the word both automatically and manually.) Repeat the procedure for the other words.

- Spell the words **pad Dan**. Reversing the reading procedure, the children *hear* the word /pad/, they segment it into individual sounds /p/ /a/ /d/, and a corresponding letter is selected from the teaching magnetic alphabet as each phoneme is segmented. Each letter is placed on the teaching magnetic board with a space between the letters: **p a d**. Children then blend the sounds and the letters are pushed together by the teacher or a child as they say the word /pad/. The magnetic letters are replaced into their position on the teacher's magnetic alphabet. Repeat the procedure for the word /Dan/. (This provides an opportunity to use the upper case version of the letter.)
- Form the letter. As in Chapter 5, teach the formation of the letter 'd', talking through the description of the procedural movement while writing the letter to support the children's cognitive processes and motor memory.

4 Practising skills acquired

Children are now in groups at their tables and are going to use their magnetic boards and letters. The display below reproduces the pupil magnetic boards with the alphabet grid. At this stage the magnetic letters on the board are **a d i m n p s t** together with a magnetic arrow to signify the left-hand side where the children will start to spell the word. Ask children to add the letter for today's sound /d/.

a	b	c	d	e	f	g	h
i	j	k	l	m			
n	o	**p**	q	r	**s t**	u	
v	w	x	y	z			
→							

The children are now going to use their magnetic boards and letters to spell words from dictation and from pictures. They can share the pupil magnetic boards and work in pairs, thus introducing the 'peer interaction element' of co-operative learning (Lyman, 1981). Presenting each word for spelling in the context of a sentence demonstrates how words have meaning.

- **Dictated word**. Children are asked to 'Spell the word **dim**. The light went **dim**. Spell the word **dim**'. After checking how the children have carried out the task and asking them to read the word, spell and write it again for reinforcement on the teacher's board, the children telling you the procedural movement for each letter. Children can confirm the spelling on their magnetic boards is the same as on the teacher's board. Children replace the letters on their magnetic boards on the grid, ready for use again.
- **Picture words**. Two pictures are normally given for each lesson. Children are given pictures of a **sad** face. You may need to discuss what kind of face it is to elicit from the children the word **sad**. Children are asked to say the word and spell it, using the same procedure as before. You will then spell and write the word on the board from the children's descriptions of the movements, as before, so that the children can check their spelling with the spelling on the board. Children replace their letters on the alphabet grid.
- The second picture for **d** is of a helicopter **pad**. To elicit the word **pad**, discuss with the children that a helicopter can land on this, a **pad**. The children then follow the same procedure as that described above to say and spell the word on their magnetic board. You will then spell and write the word on the board from the children's descriptions as before so that the children can check their own spelling. Children replace the letters on their magnetic board grids ready for use again.

Gradually, the children will be able to change from magnetic boards and letters to pencil and paper spelling, which will provide an opportunity to practise letter writing.

5 Applying skills acquired

This segment of the lesson combines the teaching of common exception (tricky) words, using them in captions and sentences together with words containing taught letters and the new letter. (In our programme, *Phonics Bug* (Watson and Johnston, 2010), these are treated as separate language sessions carried out after a set of letter sounds has been taught.)

i) Common exception (tricky) words
These words are introduced on the basis of when their constituent letters have been taught and on their degree of frequency in the English language. You might teach common exception (tricky) words other than those outlined in *Letters and Sounds* (2007) if they are needed for reading books. For example, you can teach 'said' by the time you teach the letter **d**, as all the other letter sounds will have been taught by this stage.

Common exception (tricky) words are not taught as sight words. They are taught by encouraging children to examine the words to identify known letter sounds, and to note unusual correspondences between spelling and sound and where these occur in the word (see Chapter 4 for more details on the guidance on teaching in *Letters and Sounds*, and the statutory requirements in the National Curriculum, DfE 2013). It is useful to teach the reading and spelling of these words at the same time, so that when the unusual correspondence has been pointed out for reading, children can reinforce this learning by spelling the words.

ii) Reading and spelling captions and sentences
The children have previously been introduced to **a** as a letter, it is now explained to them that **a** can also be a word. Using the letters which have been introduced up to and including the example **d**, children can be asked to read captions, e.g. 'a tin' and 'a sad man'. Captions can be dictated for children to spell with magnetic letters, e.g. 'a tin pan', and to say and spell the caption from a picture of 'a tin'.

6 Learning outcomes

You can use Table 6.1 (see above) as a guide for this plenary session. There is a column for your notes as you discuss the success criteria with the children. From your own observations you will know what the children have achieved. You now want to know *how successful the children thought they were* as you go through the expected success criteria with them and whether any specific part is causing problems. Notes you have made on the children's learning can be taken into account in the formative assessment element of the programme.

Conclude the session by singing the alphabet song with print again.

7 Ongoing formative/diagnostic assessment

Formative assessment is ongoing throughout the delivery of the programme through:

a) discussions with the pupils about what they have learnt during the session;
b) observation of how the children carry out the blending and segmenting procedures during explicit direct teaching;

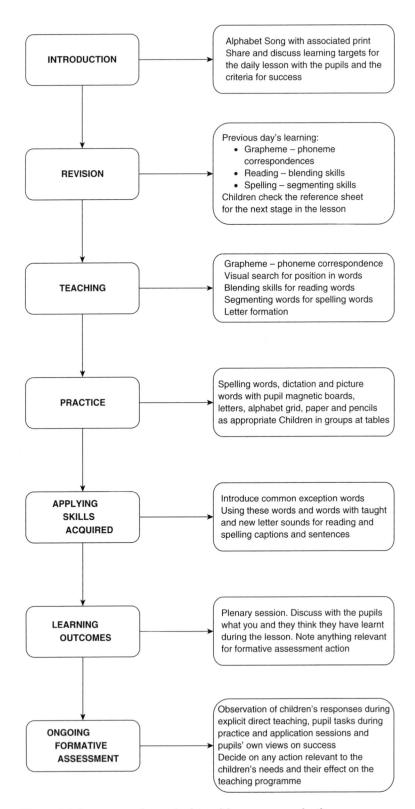

Figure 6.3 Summary of a typical teaching sequence in the programme

c) monitoring how the children carry out each of the tasks given in the Practice Sessions; and

d) checking how children apply the skills being acquired.

It would be useful to complete a record sheet after a set of letter sounds has been taught. In this way, you can identify which children might need extra support during the programme, whether some extra time might need to be taken to consolidate what has been taught before proceeding to the next lesson, and whether teaching might need to be adapted to take account of formative assessment findings (Rose, 2006).

Summary of the above sequence

Figure 6.3 illustrates the teaching sequence described above.

Variations in lesson format and integration with text reading

Some possible variations to the lesson plan

Language sessions

The consonant **d** that was used as the example for describing how to teach a lesson was taken from Phase 2 of *Letters and Sounds* (DfES, 2007). An order for teaching the Phase 2 letters in *Letters and Sounds* is given in Table 6.2, at the rate of one set of four letter sounds and one set of common exception (tricky) words per week.

Table 6.2 Phase 2 letters and high frequency/common exception words

Phase	Graphemes					High frequency/common exception words
2.1	s	a	t	p		
2.2	i	n	m	d		is, it, in, at
2.3	g	o	c	k		and
2.4	ck	e	u	r		to, the
2.5	h	b	f, ff	l, ll	ss	I, no, go

In our study in Clackmannanshire, we found that it was possible to teach blocks of four to five letter sounds in four days. The fifth day was a separate language session where we combined learning how to read and spell common exception words phonically, and to use them in captions and sentences (using previously taught letters) (Johnston and Watson, 2004). *Letters and Sounds* (DfES, 2007) suggests that Phase 2 should take about six weeks to teach, including a week for revision and consolidation.

Nearly half the sample of children came from areas of economic deprivation, but we found it was possible to teach all of Phases 2, 3 and 4 by around Easter time of Primary 1 (Reception), taking about 16 weeks. This fast pace is probably a key element of the success of the study, as the rapid learning of letter sounds soon produced a level play-ing field between the children from better and less well off areas in terms of letter sound knowledge.

Guided independent learning

In our studies, we also included a guided independent learning task, to be presented as the final part of each session for consolidation (but it could be done later in the day). When teaching **d**, our procedure was as follows:

1. On an alphabet line, the children were asked to point to the letter for /d/, the teacher indicated **d** on the alphabet, and the children said the sound.
2. The words 'stand', 'damp', 'add' and 'Adam' were presented to the children on sheets of paper, for visual search. They were asked to point to or circle the letter for /d/, saying whether it was at the beginning, mid-dle or end of the word.
3. Children practised writing the letter 'd' with pencil and paper.

Such activities will help you assess the children's learning. You can see if they can find the letter sound when it is spoken and see if they can detect the letter in printed words. You can also monitor how their letter formation skills are progressing.

Decodable books and graded readers

It is important that the phonics sessions are not perceived to be a separate entity in their own right. These phonic sessions should not be divorced from text reading, which is the practical activity where the children can apply and develop the skills they have been learning during the delivery of the phonics programme. A series of decodable readers matched to each set of taught letter sounds can be used, where the children get practice in reading captions and sentences using regular and common exception (tricky) words made up of the taught letter sounds. Grammatically such readers are likely to be progres-sive, providing experience for the children of reading:

- captions;
- one sentence to a page then two sentences to a page;
- one syllable, and then two syllable, compound words;
- nouns, proper nouns, plurals;
- pronouns, personal pronouns;
- verbs, present and past tense;
- adjectives, adverbs;
- speech bubbles leading to direct speech;
- commas, prepositions, conjunctions, questions, exclamation marks.

If such decodable readers are not available, a series of graded readers at the relevant level can be used, starting after the letters of Set 4 (see Table 6.2) have been taught. If you do this, you will need to teach any additional exception words found in the books.

The 'real' reading situation provides a further opportunity for formative assessment. The teacher can identify which child(ren) might be needing extra support, and a short-term needs group can be formed to revisit the specific aspect of the programme causing a problem.

REFLECTIVE TASK

Task 2

Try to write some linked captions and sentences for a first decodable reader using only letters from s, a, t, p, i, n, m and d, two vowels and six consonants. Indicate any art work you think might be appropriate. Analyse the text for what you think the children will have learnt.

See the end of the chapter for an example.

A SUMMARY OF **KEY POINTS**

➤ In this chapter it is explained how to integrate all the basic elements described in Chapter 5 into one sample lesson format, starting with sharing the target outcomes for the day with the pupils. It is important that the pupils know the criteria for success.

➤ The revision aspect of the lesson format is described in detail, followed by the teaching of the new letter sound for word reading, spelling and letter formation, using whole class direct teaching.

➤ To practise and apply the skills acquired, the children now work in pairs with pupil magnetic boards and letters, thus setting the scene for co-operative learning. As well as spelling dictated and picture words, the phonic reading and spelling of common exception (tricky) words is introduced together with reading captions and sentences.

➤ The learning outcomes aspect of the lesson relates to the sharing of the day's targets. From your own observations using formative assessment, you will know what the children have achieved and whether there are individual needs to be addressed. What is important now is how successful the children think they have been.

➤ A summary of the aforementioned teaching sequence in the programme is displayed in Figure 6.3.

➤ The importance of including decodable or graded readers is also discussed in some detail to integrate the phonic sessions and 'real reading'.

REFLECTIVE TASK

Task 2 answers

Words from two sets of letters s, a, t, p, i, n, m, d							
s	a	t	p	i	n	m	d
sap	a	tap	Pat pat	in	Nan	map	dim
sat	an	tin	pan	is	Nip nip	mat	din
sip	as	tip	pin	it	nap	man	dip
sit	at	Tim	Pip pip	imp	Nana	mats	Dan
sip	am	taps	pit		nips	maps	Dad

(Continued)

(Continued)

Sid	Ann	tips	Pam				dims
sits	add	tins	pad				dips
sips	and		pads				
	ant		pans				
	ants		pins				
	Anna		pips				
			pats				
			Papa				

The following are examples of linked captions and sentences using words from the above table. Note that no common exception words have been introduced yet but reference is made to relevant high frequency words, namely is, it, in, at. Suggested appropriate art work and grammatical features are included.

Caption/Sentence	Art work	Learning potential
Tim and Anna	Boy and girl playing in the garden with a 'Wendy' house.	Capital letters for names. Introducing conjunction 'and'.
Tim, Anna and Pip	Pip, a playful kitten, added to the above scene.	Introducing a comma between Tim and Anna.
Tim taps a tin.	Same scene but with Tim tapping a tin with a drum stick. Another empty tin lying beside him.	Introducing a sentence, starts with a capital letter and ends with a full stop. 'taps' as a verb. 'a' as a word and an adjective.
Anna taps a pan.	Same scene but with Anna tapping a pan with a drum stick. Another empty pan lying beside her.	As above.
Pip sits in a pan.	Same scene as above but with Pip sitting in what was the empty pan.	As above. Introducing preposition 'in'.
Pip sits in a tin.	Same scene as above but with Pip sitting in what was the empty tin. The pan is lying upside down as Pip tipped it over.	As above.
Tim taps Pip's tin.	Same scene as above. Tim has left his tin and comes over to Pip's tin to tap it with his drumstick. Pip scampers out of the tin.	As above. Introducing the use of an apostrophe.
Anna and Tim pat Pip.	Scene now with two tins and two pans and two drum sticks lying about. Pip sitting beside Anna and Tim who are stroking and patting the kitten.	Concluding sentence. A title for the linked captions and sentences might be 'Tim, Anna and Pip'.

REFERENCES REFERENCES **REFERENCES** REFERENCES **REFERENCES** REFERENCES

DfE (2013) *The National Curriculum in England*. London: DfE. https://www.gov.uk/government/publications/national-curriculum-in-england-framework-for-key-stages-1-to-4 (retrieved 17 March 2014).

DfES (2007) *Letters and Sounds*. London: DfES. https://www.gov.uk/government/publications/letters-and-sounds (retrieved 27 August 2014).

Johnston, R.S. and Watson, J. (2004) Accelerating the development of reading, spelling and phonemic awareness. *Reading and Writing*, 17(4), 327–57.

Lyman, F. (1981) Think, Pair, Share. www.eazhull.org.uk/nlc/think,_pair,_share.htm (retrieved 2l January 2007).

Rose, J. (2006) *Independent review of the teaching of early reading: Final Report*. Nottingham: DfES. http://webarchive.nationalarchives.gov.uk/20100408085953/http://standards.dcsf.gov.uk/phonics/rosereview/ (retrieved 27 August 2014).

Watson, J.E and Johnston, R.S. (2010) *Phonics Bug*. Harlow: Pearson.

7
Teaching Phases 3 to 6 of *Letters and Sounds*

Learning objectives

In this chapter, you will learn how to:

- teach a Phase 5 synthetic phonics lesson;
- identify consonant digraphs, vowel digraphs and adjacent consonants;
- visually divide words into syllables for reading;
- teach syllable blending for word reading;
- segment words into syllables and then phonemes for spelling;
- add prefix and suffix morphemes to root words;
- dictate sentences including the taught graphemes, and high frequency and common exception (tricky) words;
- assess the children's learning against stated criteria for success;
- use the detailed daily lesson plans as forward planning for the weekly plan, which in turn fits in with the long-term curriculum plan.

TEACHERS' STANDARDS

3. Demonstrate good subject and curriculum knowledge
4. Plan and teach well structured lessons
5. Adapt teaching to respond to the strengths and needs of all pupils
6. Make accurate and productive use of assessment

Phases 3 and 4 of *Letters and Sounds*: Beyond single letter–sound correspondences

Phase 3: less frequent letter sounds and the introduction of consonant and vowel digraphs

In Chapter 6 (p.81), we showed you the *Letters and Sounds* (DfES, 2007) order for teaching consonants and vowels in Phase 2 of the programme. Phase 2 covers the first 19 letters of the alphabet, i.e. s,a,t,p,i,n,m,d,g,o,c,k,ck,e,u,r,h,b,f,ff,l,ll,ss.

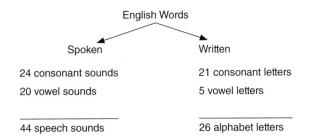

Figure 7.1 Speech sounds in relation to letters of the alphabet (Morris, 1990)

Although **ck**, **ff**, **ll** and **ss** consist of two graphemes, the phoneme correspondence is /k/, /f/, /l/, and /s/. *Letters and Sounds* suggests that Phase 2 should take about six weeks to teach, allowing a week for revision and consolidation.

When compiling such a sequence, the authors of *Letters and Sounds* will have been aware of the need to separate letters of graphic similarity, as they might confuse some children. It might be useful for you to know that there are clearly defined 'groups of letters with graphic similarity' (Dunn-Rankin, 1968) such as:

- e, a, s, c, o
- f, l, t, k, i, h
- b, d, p, o, g, h
- n, u, m, w, h

The letters **j**, **q**, **v**, **x** and **z** were excluded in Dunn-Rankin's research because of their infrequent use in primary readers. *Letters and Sounds* introduces these five letters (together with **w** and **y**) quite late on, as the first two sets of letters for Phase 3. This is not problematical if children progress rapidly to Phase 3 work after around six weeks of Phase 2 phonics teaching, as suggested in *Letters and Sounds*. However, if children spend most of Reception doing Phase 2 work, there will be a lot of words that cannot be taught phonically, and they will only be able to use a restricted range of decodable readers.

Up to this point, children have learnt that one letter stands for one sound. However, in English, there are more speech sounds than there are letters of the alphabet. Morris (1990) illustrates this in Figure 7.1.

Phase 3 introduces the idea that some sounds are connected to more than one letter, e.g. the letters **c** and **h** as in /church/, and **s** and **h** as in /shop/, come together to sound /ch/ and /sh/ respectively. These are known as consonant digraphs. Vowel digraphs such as **a** and **i** come together to sound the long vowel sound /ā/ as in /pail/ and **oi** as in /coin/. It is common practice to teach phonics in this order: the simple consonant and vowel correspondences, then the more complex consonant and vowel digraphs. These digraphs are introduced in Phase 3 when all the single letter sounds have been taught. The progression for Phase 3 is shown in Table 7.1, in which each line represents one week's teaching.

Letters and Sounds (DfES, 2007) suggests that Phases 2 and 3 together should take about 18 weeks maximum to complete, which allows time for practice and consolidation.

Table 7.1 Phase 3 letters, consonant digraphs, vowel digraphs and high frequency/ common exception words

Phase 3	Sets of letters (to be taught also in the context of words)				High frequency/common exception words
3.1	j	v	w	x	Revise preceding words
3.2	y	z,zz	qu		he, she
	Consonant digraphs, vowel digraphs				
3.3	ch	sh	th **th**	ng	we, me, be
3.4	ai	ee	igh	oa	was
3.5	oo **oo**	ar	or	ur	my
3.6	ow (cow)	oi	ear	air	you
3.7	ure	er			they
3.8	**Consolidation**				her
3.9	Teach: reading and spelling of high frequency/ common exception words. Practise: all GPCs*; letter names; blending for reading; segmentation for spelling; two syllable words; reading and writing captions and sentences				all
3.10					are
3.11	More consolidation if necessary or move on to Phase 4				

* Grapheme to phoneme correspondences

Phase 4: adjacent consonants

In Chapter 4, we showed that Phase 4 covers adjacent consonants (or consonant blends), that is, a sequence of consonants at the beginning or end of words, e.g. <u>cl</u>ap, <u>str</u>ing, po<u>st</u>. The purpose of Phase 4 is described by *Letters and Sounds* as being 'to consolidate children's knowledge of graphemes in reading and spelling words containing adjacent consonants' (p107). A bank of suggested words is provided from which you can select those needed for an activity. In Table 7.2 we have selected one word for each

Table 7.2 Phase 4 adjacent consonants and high frequency/common exception words

Phase 4	Adjacent consonants				High frequency/ common exception words
4.1	desk	wasp	best	shift	said, so, he, she, we
4.2	skip	spot	step	spoil	have, like, some, come
4.3	Consolidation Teach: reading and spelling of high frequency/common exception words. Practise: Phases 2/3 graphemes; reading adjacent consonant words; spelling adjacent consonant words; reading and writing sentences				were, there, little, one, all, are
4.4					do, when, out, what

day as an example, but bear in mind that Annex B of *The Primary Framework for Literacy and Mathematics* (Primary National Strategy, 2006) says that you should not to teach lists of similar words such as 'best', 'nest', 'vest' in one lesson. One line represents one week's teaching.

You will see again that a few weeks are available for consolidation, but the teaching of common exception (tricky) and high frequency words has been speeded up from Phase 3. Phases 2 to 4 together are expected to take a maximum of 24 weeks teaching according to *Letters and Sounds*, to be completed before the end of Reception (Primary 1). In our study in Clackmannanshire, we found that children could read words containing adjacent consonants from very early on, so there is no need to have a separate Phase 4; the advantage of teaching such items early on again lies in the wider range of reading material to which children can be introduced. Overall, the work in Phases 2 to 4 was taught in 16 weeks in Clackmannanshire (Johnston and Watson, 2004).

REFLECTIVE TASK

Task 1

Try to complete the table below with words that fit into the categories of initial adjacent consonants (ccvc words), final adjacent consonants (cvcc words), and initial and final adjacent consonants (ccvcc, cccvcc, and ccvccc words).

ccvc words	cvcc words	ccvcc words	cccvcc words	ccvccc words
frog	lamp	chest	thrust	brunch

Phase 5

In *Letters and Sounds* (DfES, 2007), this phase is to be covered in Year 1 (Primary 2).

Spelling alternatives and a sample Phase 5 lesson

Phase 5 introduces children to the complexities of the English spelling system. Some vowel sounds can be represented in alternative ways, e.g. the long vowel sound /ā/ can be represented by **ai** (train), **ay** (play), **a–e** (gate), **eigh** (eight), **ey** (obey) and **ei** (reins); these are known as spelling alternatives. The new graphemes for reading for Phase 5, in weeks 1 to 4, are shown in Table 7.3. It is recommended that you teach about four per week, so a line represents one week's teaching.

We are now going to show you how to teach the vowel digraph **oy** from Phase 5 (see Table 7.3), using the basic Phase 2 lesson plan described in Chapter 6 (where we used the letter **d**).

Introduction	Share the daily targets and criteria for success with the children Use your structured guide or lesson notes to prompt you for the sequence of the lesson Display an outline sheet[1] for the children's benefit
Revision	Revisit the /oi/ sound from Phase 3 (which is the same sound as for oy) Ask the children to: • read the words (blending if needed): **oil joint soil coins** • segment and spell the words for you to write on the board: **coil boil spoil join** • spell previous high frequency words: **said, so, come, like**
Teach	'oy' sounds the same as the previous learned sound /oi/; pronounce and find the vowel digraph position in words: **toy employ annoy joy** the syllable blending strategy for reading two-syllable words[2]: **enjoy** the syllable blending strategy for spelling two-syllable words[2]: **ahoy** common exception and high frequency words, reading and spelling: **oh their**
Practice	reading **oy** words: **oyster royal** spelling dictated words: **joy tomboy** spelling picture words: **boy toys**
Apply	Read the sentence: **We enjoy going to the play park.** Write the sentence: **Joy and Roy can come with us.**
Assess learning outcomes against success criteria	Plenary session with the children. From your own observations you will know what the children have achieved. You now want to know what the children think they have achieved. Would they give themselves a happy face or a sad face? If a sad face, perhaps this is where there is a problem to be addressed. Children should be able to: • give the correct sound for given grapheme; • write the grapheme correctly for given sounds; • use the blending strategy for reading two-syllable words;
	• use the blending strategy for spelling two-syllable words; • read a sentence which includes a high frequency/common exception word; • write a sentence which includes a high frequency/common exception word, forming the letters correctly.
Ongoing formative assessment	From assessing the learning indicated above, you can identify which children might be needing extra support during the programme, whether some extra time might need to be taken to consolidate what has been taught before proceeding to the next lesson, and whether your teaching might need to be adapted.

[1]Figure 6.2 in Chapter 6 gives guidance on how to design a chart for the children that outlines the sections of the lesson, so they can see how the lesson is proceeding.

[2]See the section below, 'Syllabification' (p. 92), for a description of how we would teach children to blend multi-syllablic words for reading, and to segment them for spelling.

Figure 7.2 Example of actual lesson plan for Phase 5

Table 7.3 Phase 5 vowel and consonant digraphs (graphemes), high frequency/common exception words

Phase 5	Vowel and consonant digraphs (to be taught also in the context of words)				High frequency/common exception words
5.1	ay	oy	wh	a–e	oh, their
5.2	ou	ir	ph	e–e	people, Mr, Mrs
5.3	ie (pie)	ue (Sue)	ew (new)	i–e	looked, called, asked
5.4	ea (eat) zh (treasure)	aw au (Paul)	oe (toe)	o–e u–e (tube)	Revise preceding words

Alternative pronunciations for graphemes

For weeks 5 to 7 of Phase 5, *Letters and Sounds* (DfES, 2007) concentrates on common alternative pronunciations for graphemes, for example, the soft 'c' as in 'ice' and the soft 'g' as in 'ginger'. Examples of the alternative pronunciations for graphemes recommended for teaching by *Letters and Sounds* are given in Table 7.4.

Table 7.4 Phase 5 graphemes with alternative pronunciations, high frequency/common exception words

Phase 5	Graphemes with alternative pronunciations (to be taught also in the context of words)				High frequency/common exception words
5.5	'i' (kind)	'ow' (blow)	'y' (by) (very)	'o' (cold)	eyes, any, many, because
5.6	'ie' (field)	'ch' (chef) (school)	'c' (pencil)	'ea' (bread)	again, once, please, friends
5.7	'ou' (could) (shoulder) (you)	'g' (ginger)	'er' (her)	'u' (put) 'a' (what)	work, where, different, laughed, water, thought, through, mouse, who

Alternative spellings for phonemes

For weeks 8 to 30 of Phase 5, *Letters and Sounds* continues with:

- practising and consolidating previous learning;
- reading and spelling words with adjacent consonants;
- reading and spelling both high frequency words and multi-syllabic words;
- reading and writing sentences.

In addition, the concept of alternative spellings for phonemes is now introduced. For example, the target phoneme is /m/ but the spelling is 'lamb', the target sound is /z/ but the spelling is 'cheese'. *Letters and Sounds* provides banks of words and sentences which can be used in the same way as we demonstrated in the lesson for teaching the vowel digraph **oy** (Figure 7.2, p. 90).

Syllabification

During Phases 2 to 4, the children will have learnt to work with individual letters, sounding and blending successive letters to read words, and segmenting phonemes to spell words. Even when words of more than one syllable were introduced, e.g. 'wigwam', 'zebra', 'anorak', the children will have sounded and blended individual successive letters for reading. However, in this Phase 5 the children now need to learn how to blend syllables together for reading. They also need to learn how to segment words into syllables, before segmenting them in turn into phonemes for spelling. In this section we will outline how we would teach these elements.

A syllable is a word or part of a word that can be spoken independently, e.g. 'alphabet' has three syllables, **al/ pha/ bet**. Recognition of syllables, and breaking words into syllables, is important for both reading and spelling. Pupils need to know that:

- all words have at least one syllable;
- each syllable has one vowel sound (vowel digraphs counting as one vowel);
- long words are made up of short syllables;
- syllables can be one letter or a group of letters, one of which must be a vowel sound (including 'y' used as a vowel).

REFLECTIVE TASK

Task 1 Syllabification

Insert each word from the list of words in the following table into the appropriate column and indicate the syllable splits in the words.

See the end of the chapter for the answers.

Words			1 syllable	2 syllables	3 syllables
Ruth	Alison	Philip	Ruth	Phil/ ip	Al/ is/ on
circle	hexagon	cube			
elephant	horse	rabbit			
apple	celery	grape			
barbecue	quiche	kebab			

From the above activity, you will have noticed, for example, that 'cube' is only one syllable. This is because silent 'e', although a vowel, does not count as a syllable. There are recognised rules for where to split words into syllables, which you will find in Appendix 5.

In Phase 5, the children need to learn to tackle multi-syllabic words for reading and spelling by breaking them down into their component syllables. We would teach these skills to children by:

1. showing them how to divide words into syllables visually for reading;
2. showing them how to divide syllables auditorily into syllables (and then into phonemes) for spelling;
3. showing them how to apply the skills in 2 when writing to dictation sentences containing multi-syllabic words.

1. Reading words of more than one syllable, children will:

SEE the printed word and will need to be able to:	**bedroom**
1. separate the target printed word into syllables	bed/ room
2. sound and blend successive letters of each syllable	/b/ /e/ /d/ -> /bed/ /r/ /oo/ /m/ -> /room/
3. sound and blend successive syllables to read the word	/bed/ /room/ -> bedroom
4. read the whole two-syllable word	**bedroom**

2. Spelling words of more than one syllable, children will:

HEAR the target word and will need to be able to:	
1. pronounce the target word	/bedroom/
2. break the word into syllables, and pronounce each syllable	/bed/ /room/
3. sound and write the successive letters of each syllable, and then blend them to check the letter order	/b/ /e/ /d/ -> /bed/ /r/ /oo/ /m/ -> /room/
4. sound and blend the successive syllables to spell and say	/bed/ /room/ -> bedroom
5. spell the target word orally using the letter names	'b' 'e' 'd' 'r' 'o' 'o' 'm' spells **bedroom**

3. Dictation of sentences

In our programme *Phonics Bug* (Watson and Johnston, 2010) we suggest a procedure you can follow for the dictation of a sentence, namely:

1. Revise the specific aspect being stressed within the sentence, e.g. the taught graphemes, common exception words, multi-syllabic words and so on. If the purpose of the sentence is to include a word with more than one syllable, you may feel you need to go over the procedure we described above for breaking up the word into the syllables. (If you use the board to demonstrate this, remember to clear it before starting the activity.)
2. Slowly and distinctly dictate the sentence to the children.
3. Ask them to repeat the sentence together.
4. Dictate the sentence again and ask the children to write it. *Pause to give the children time to do this.*
5. Ask some of the children to assist you in writing the sentence on the board by telling you which letters to write for the words.
6. Ask a child to read the completed sentence.
7. You and the children can compare their sentences with the one on the board.

Phase 6: Introducing morphemes

In Phase 6, children learn to think about segmenting words into meaningful units, i.e. **morphemes**. Morphemes are the smallest units of meaning in language and consist of one or more phonemes. A root or base word can stand alone, and is a morpheme in its own right (e.g. 'turn'). It can have a prefix (e.g. '<u>re</u>turn') or a suffix (e.g. 'turn<u>ing</u>') or both a prefix and a suffix (e.g. '<u>re</u>turn<u>ing</u>'). If children learn to recognise larger segments in unfamiliar words, such as morphemes, this will aid the fluency and automaticity of their word reading.

Suffixes

A suffix is a morpheme which can be a letter or a group of letters and is added after a word; below are examples of suffix morphemes attached to root words.

- **-s** (dog/dogs)   provides information – there is more than one dog
- **-es** (box/boxes)   provides information – there is more than one box
- **-ing** (waiting   provides information – this is happening in the present tense
- **-ed** (waited)   provides information – this happened in the past tense

Table 7.5 shows some more examples of how suffixes can be added to root words.

Table 7.5 Suffix morphemes

Suffix	What it means	Examples
-s	This makes the word plural and means more than one	**star/stars**
-es (after s, ss)	This makes the word plural and means more than one	**bus/buses** **class/classes**
-es (after ch, sh, tch)	This makes the word plural and means more than one	**arch/arches** **wish/wishes** **watch/watches**
-es (after x, z/zz)	This makes the word plural and means more than one	**box/boxes** **buzz/buzzes**
-ed	In the past	**splash/splashed**
-ing	Doing now in the present	**splash/splashing**

Prefixes

A prefix morpheme can be a letter or group of letters such as 're' and 'un' put before a word. It is usually joined to the word to change its meaning e.g. 'return' (see Table 7.6).

Table 7.6 Prefix morphemes

Prefix	What it means	Examples
re-	again	**build/rebuild**
un-	not	**known/unknown**

Pace of delivery of programme

Letters and Sounds (DfES, 2007) envisages the following timetable for Phases 2 to 6. Phases 2 to 4 should be completed in Reception year (Primary 1), and Phase 5 should be taught during Year 1 (Primary 2), prior to children sitting the Phonics Check. Phase 6 is intended to be taught in Year 2 (Primary 3). This latter phase will lend itself to further consolidation of teaching and learning, with reading becoming more fluent and automatic; here children will learn about word structure and spelling, laying the foundation for Key Stage 2 (Primaries 4 to 7). This is the pace we suggest in our programme *Phonics Bug* (Watson and Johnston, 2010). However, the pace of phonics teaching can be moderated according to the needs of the class, as you may have a class that needs extra time for the consolidation for their learning.

We have shown that one lesson format can be used on a daily basis throughout the programme. From the first example, using the single consonant **d** and one-syllable CVC words (shown in Chapter 6), to the second example, using the vowel digraph **oy** with multi-syllablic words (this chapter), you can identify the progression:

- from sounding and blending *letters* to sounding and blending *syllables* and *morphemes*;
- from using magnetic letters to using pencil and paper for dictation and spelling;
- building-up of the learning of common exception (tricky) and high frequency words;
- learning alternative spellings for phonemes;
- moving from reading captions to sentences, to connected sentences and text.

The continued use of decodable/graded readers will provide opportunities for children to practise reading and to develop fluency in reading.

Curriculum implications

Link to dictionary skills

We found that the fast pace used in our studies meant that many other aspects of the curriculum could be introduced earlier. For example, the children had knowledge about the alphabet, both lower and upper case letters and alphabetic order, right from the start of school. It was found therefore that this knowledge could serve as a foundation for learning dictionary skills at an earlier stage than would previously have been the case. Activities such as placing words in alphabetical order, and using words beginning with different letters, served as preparation for being able to start looking up words in a dictionary, and learning about the function of a dictionary. We have included such activities in our programme *Phonics Bug* (Watson and Johnston, 2010).

Link to school and class forward planning

We find that with our programme, the structure and format is such that it lends itself not only to **detailed weekly planning**, but also to **detailed daily planning**. The ongoing formative assessment element means that children needing extra support can easily be identified and given support within the class. At some stage, a Support for Learning (SfL) teacher may need to be involved. If so, an **individual learning programme** can be devised for joint implementation between the SfL teacher and the class teacher. You will be able to read about such co-operation in the Case Study in Chapter 8.

A SUMMARY OF **KEY POINTS**

➢ As there are more speech sounds than there are letters of the alphabet (Morris, 1990), the concept of consonant and vowel digraphs, e.g. 'chop', 'coat', is discussed.

➢ We includes tables illustrating the *Letters and Sounds* (DfES, 2007) order for teaching consonant and vowel digraphs and common exception (tricky) and high frequency words in Phase 3, and adjacent consonants in Phase 4.

➢ A sample implementation of a lesson demonstrating how to teach a Phase 5 vowel digraph is included (using the same format as the basic lesson plan for teaching a Phase 2 single letter in Chapter 6).

➢ We include tables illustrating an order for teaching the alternative pronunciations for graphemes, the alternative spellings for phonemes, and the common exception (tricky) and high frequency words listed in Letters and Sounds (DfES, 2007) for Phase 5.

➢ We cover the concepts of syllabification needed for Phase 5, where the recognition of syllables and the breaking words into syllables are critical skills for both reading and spelling. Strategies for reading and spelling words of more than one syllable are set out, as is a procedure for dictating sentences for children to write.

➢ In Phase 6, children learn to think about segmenting words into meaningful units. The concept of morphemes is introduced; root (or base) words, prefix and suffix morphemes are described.

➢ We explain that dictionary skills can be introduced at an earlier stage than with previous programmes.

➢ The impact of a very structured phonics programme on school planning procedures is discussed.

REFLECTIVE TASK

Task 1 answers: Syllabification

Insert each word from the list of words in the following table into the appropriate column and indicate the syllable splits in the words.

Words			1 syllable	2 syllables	3 syllables
Ruth	Alison	Philip	Ruth	Phil/ip	Al/is/on
circle	hexagon	cube	cube	cir/cle	hex/a/gon
elephant	horse	rabbit	horse	rab/bit	el/e/phant

| apple | celery | grape | grape | ap/ple | cel/e/ry |
| barbecue | quiche | kebab | quiche | ke/bab | bar/be/cue |

REFERENCES REFERENCES **REFERENCES** REFERENCES REFERENCES REFERENCES

DfES (2007) *Letters and Sounds*. London: DfES.https://www.gov.uk/government/publications/letters-and-sounds (retrieved 27 August 2014).

Dunn-Rankin, P. (1968) The similarity of lower case letters of the English Alphabet. *Journal of Verbal Learning and Verbal Behaviour*, 7, 990–5.

Johnston, R.S and Watson, J. (2004) Accelerating the development of reading, spelling and phonemic awareness. *Reading and Writing*, 17(4), 327–57.

Morris, J. (1990) *The Morris-Montessori Word List*. London: The London Montessori Centre Ltd.

Primary National Strategy (2006) *The Primary Framework for Literacy and Mathematics: Guidance for practitioners and teachers on progression and pace in the teaching of phonics (Annex B Outline of Progression).* London: DfES. http://www.standards.dfes.gov.uk/primary/features/primary/pri_fwk_corepapers/ (retrieved 27 August 2014).

Watson, J.E. and Johnston, R.S (2010) *Phonics Bug*. Harlow: Pearson.

8
The Phonics Check and how to assess and diagnose reading problems

Learning objectives

In this chapter, you will learn:

- about the rationale for the Phonics Check;
- how to assess children's phonic difficulties, and how to support their learning to improve their phonic skills;
- how all of these approaches were used to help a child with special educational needs achieve a very good standard of word reading and spelling performance.

TEACHERS' STANDARDS

3. Demonstrate good subject and curriculum knowledge
5. Adapt teaching to respond to the strengths and needs of all pupils
6. Make accurate and productive use of assessment

The Phonics Screening Check: a statutory phonics check for England

Later in the chapter we will tell you about Anthony, a boy who started school a year later than his classmates because of his learning difficulties. With a great deal of support he was able to read words appropriately for his age when he left primary school. Throughout the long period of learning support he received, we were able to monitor his developing phonics skills by giving him nonwords (pseudowords) to read. Although we asked him to read words to assess his level of reading ability compared with national norms, we also needed to know what areas of phonics he was good at and what were the areas where he needed to do further work. When we gave him lists of words to read we could not be sure how he had read them. Some words might have been read by phonic synthesis, and some by sight; those words recognised by sight might not have had a secure phonic underpinning. The solution to this issue of finding out what phonic weaknesses a child has, in order to target extra tuition, is to ask them to read nonwords. For example, with Anthony we found that there was a stage where he could blend consonant-vowel-consonant nonwords very well, but he had problems with adjacent consonants, e.g. 'sp'. A year later, after a targeted intervention, he had little difficulty with adjacent consonants at the beginning and end of words.

These sorts of improvements underlie the rationale behind the UK government's decision to introduce a statutory Phonics Screening Check at the end of the second year at school.

The Check contains both words and nonwords and it was administered for the first time to children in Year 1 in 2012 (with children not meeting the expected standard retaking it in 2013). The Department for Education (DfE) (2013a) stresses this is not a reading test but a test of phonic knowledge.

The Check is divided into two sections. Section 1 covers Phases 2 to 4, where children are taught all of the single letter sounds, some consonant and vowel digraphs, and words containing adjacent consonants; according to *Letters and Sounds* (DfES, 2007) these phases should be covered by the end of Reception. Section 2 is designed to assess Year 1 learning, which covers Phase 5 phonics. In this phase children learn new graphemes, and also that some vowel spellings have alternative pronunciations, and that some vowels have alternative spellings.

The Standards and Testing Agency (2012) has produced an outline of the structure of the Phonics Screening Check, which can be used as a guide for teaching. Overall, the Check contains 40 items, of which 20 are words and 20 are pseudowords. In Section 1, there are 12 pseudowords and 8 real words. Examples of the word structures that can be used are CVC, VCC, CCVC and CVCC; however, it should be noted that these are phonemic structures not orthographic/spelling structures (for example, V can mean two vowels, i.e. a vowel digraph). All of the single letters may be used, and there can be some consonant digraphs (i.e. ch, ck, ff, ll, ng, sh, ss, th, zz) and some frequent and consistent vowel digraphs (i.e. ar, ee, oi, oo, or). In Section 2 more complex structures can be used: CCVCC, CCCVC, CCCVCC words, two syllable words, and some additional consonant digraphs (i.e. ph, wh). This section also includes vowel digraphs (i.e. a-e, ai, au, aw, ay, ea, e-e, ew, i-e, ie, ir, oa, o-e, ou, ow, oy, ue, u-e, ur), which are some of the most difficult structures children have to read; you can see that this section includes split vowel digraphs and some vowel digraphs with variable pronunciations. There are also some vowel trigraphs (i.e. air, igh). Table 8.1 shows a sample screening check that the Standards and Testing Agency (2012) has produced. The actual check items are printed for the children in the Sassoon Infant typeface, 48 pitch.

It can be seen that for each section the pseudowords are presented first, followed by the words; this helps reduce the chance that children will try to read the pseudowords as words, though inevitably some will be read in this way. However, this will have been taken into account in the standardisation of the check. In 2012 and 2013, the expected level of performance was set at 32 items out of 40 correct. The percentage of children reaching the expected level in 2012 was 58% (DfE, 2013b). The children who did not reach the expected level in Year 1 re-sat the check in Year 2. By the end of Year 2, 85% of the pupils were above threshold on the check, as a further 27% were now performing at the expected level.

For those not meeting the expected level, this sample Phonics Check can be used to provide information to the class teacher about what catch-up work it would be helpful for the children to do. It is a safe bet that many will be struggling to read the vowel digraphs at this stage! However, some children will still be having problems in identifying the single letter sounds correctly, blending adjacent consonants, and recognising some consonant digraphs. Children in Year 1 not studying Phase 5 phonics, where they get extensive coverage of vowel digraphs, will be at a disadvantage on the check.

By 2013 (DfE, 2013b) the proportion of children reaching the expected standard had increased to 69%, 73% of girls and 65% of boys, showing an 11% increase from the

**Table 8.1 Sample Phonics Screening Check from Standards
and Testing Agency (2012)**

Section 1	Section 2
tox	voo
bim	jound
vap	terg
ulf	fape
geck	snemp
chom	blurst
tord	spron
thazz	stroft
blan	day
steck	slide
hild	newt
quemp	phone
shin	blank
gang	trains
week	strap
chill	scribe
grit	rusty
start	finger
best	dentist
hooks	starling

previous year. Of particular interest is that 69% of children whose first language was not English met the expected standard. It was also found that pupils from an Indian background had 80% of children meeting the expected standard, but travellers of Irish Heritage and those from a Gypsy/Roma background scored 28% and 23% respectively. When the data were split by eligibility for free school meals, 56% of those who were eligible met the required standard, whereas of those not eligible 72% met the standard. For children having special educational needs (SEN), 32% performed at the required standard, whereas 76% of non SEN pupils met the standard.

The assessment of phonic difficulties

We have developed two Phonics Checks for our research (Hull Diagnostic Phonics Checks 1 and 2, Appendix 6), to target catch-up work for children not meeting the expected level in the government's Phonics Check. The tests are paired in the sense that the phonic structures tested by words in Check 1 are tested by nonwords in Check 2, and vice versa. Section 1 contains the phonics taught in Phases 2 to 4 in *Letters and Sounds*

(DfES, 2007), and Section 2 contains Phase 5 phonics. We have found that these tests are somewhat harder than the government's Phonics Check, as they test Phase 5 more fully; for example, there is a wider range of vowel digraphs (some of which have alternative pronunciations), and so far 'dge', 'tch', 'wh', 'ge' and 'ce' have not appeared in the Phonics Checks. This is because our tests were designed with an eye to formative assessment; the only Phase 5 aspect not covered is silent letters, e.g. 'kn'. Mean performance on the government's Phonics Check for the children in our study was 29.63 out of 40 correct in June of 2012, when they were in Year 1. Our tests were carried out in December of Year 2: mean performance for the children who read the items on Hull Diagnostic Phonics Check 1 was 26.90 out of 40, and mean performance for the children doing Hull Diagnostic Phonics Check 2 was 23.90 (Johnston *et al.*, in preparation).

These diagnostic phonics checks can be used for formative assessment. Section 1 of the checks can be used with children nearing the end of Reception, and Section 2 can be used towards the end of Year 1 (but of course the benchmark of 32 items correct over both sections should not be applied as these tests are harder than the government's Phonics Check). They can also be used to diagnose the learning needs of slower learners who have not met the expected level in Year 1.

However, it is very beneficial to carry out formative assessment from earlier on in phonics teaching, starting with assessing letter-sound learning.

Letter sound learning

The first thing to assess is the children's knowledge of letter sounds, as these are the building blocks of phonics. For some children this basic level of learning can be very difficult. You can usefully assess the child's ability to read the letters and to write them to dictation. In order to help such children learn the letter sounds, it may be beneficial to teach them mnemonics such as characters associated with the letters, or distinctive hand and sound actions, as well as plenty of work forming the letters. All of these activities will help consolidate the letters and their sounds in memory. However, some children will remember the mnemonics and not the sounds when you test their letter knowledge, so *Letters and Sounds* (DfES, 2007) advises that this work should be time limited.

We have found that it is not necessary for children to have complete mastery of the letter sounds that they have been taught in order to continue with the phonics programme; each letter will be repeated over and over in the next phonics phase, so this will reinforce their learning. For example, the children who do not know all of the 19 letters taught in Phase 2 can nevertheless progress to Phase 3, where they will continually meet these letters again. This will have the advantage that they can now be exposed to a wider range of printed words than can be made up from the Phase 2 letters. The aim of a synthetic phonics scheme is to teach children to recognise words rapidly by sight after a few decodings using a sounding and blending approach. This is why children do not need a separate strand of being taught high frequency words by sight without phonic analysis; however they do need to be exposed to a wide set of words. If some children spend a long time in Phase 2 they will be exposed to a narrow range of words, and will have an impoverished reading experience. We have found that slower learners can stay in the class programme, and can be helped with extra teaching in small groups so that they can keep up with the class.

Blending for reading and segmenting for spelling

Some children are very slow to learn to sound and blend for reading or to segment spoken words for spelling, even when they know quite a few letter sounds. We do not recommend holding a child back from the classroom phonics programme until she or he can blend and segment, as we have found it beneficial for slower learning children to stay in the class programme, where they get plenty of exposure to sounding and blending, and to printed words. Joining in with these activities will remind them that when reading unfamiliar words they need to look at letter sounds for useful information, tracking from left to right to decode the words. Staying in the class programme will also aid their vocabulary development. However, they can do additional work with other slower learners at other times during the day, to help them keep up.

Assessing blending skills

We recommend that to assess blending skills the children read nonwords (i.e. pseudowords) that test the knowledge of what is taught in each phase. The reason we recommend nonwords is that if you show the child real words these may be words that the child has learnt to recognise by sight without having grasped the phonic skill that you are checking. Early blending skills can be assessed in Phases 2 and 3 by asking the children to read simple one-syllable CVC nonwords, such as 'kug', and two-syllable CVCCVC nonwords, e.g. 'minlan' (see Appendix 7, section a). Later on, the Phase 4 list for adjacent consonants can be used (section b), and the vowel digraphs list can be used for Phase 5 (section c); by this stage the problems are more likely to be due to lack of knowledge of the grapheme–phoneme correspondences rather than difficulties in blending. It is very useful to take notes on how children tackle these tasks, to get an idea of what their problems are.

- If the children give you a real word, they may not have understood the task, in which case you can read a few nonwords for them to show them what is wanted.
- If they still cannot read any nonwords, but in other tests you have found that they know the letter sounds, they may have got the idea that they can read an unfamiliar word from its visual appearance without working systematically through the letter sounds.
- If the children go sequentially through the letter sounds and are still not be able to come up with a pronunciation of the nonword, then they are having difficulty in blending.

We recommend with all of these difficulties that the child spends some time pronouncing nonwords to master the principle of sounding and blending, as only a phonic approach will lead to a successful outcome with nonwords, whereas any real words used may already be known by the child.

Assessing segmentation skills

You can assess the children's ability to segment spoken words in two ways:

a) pronouncing a word, asking them to repeat it, and then asking them to tell you the sounds from first to last;
b) doing the above, and asking them to select the appropriate magnetic letters.

They may only be able to tell you the first sound, they may miss sounds, or they may get the sounds out of sequence. If this is the problem, you can reinforce segmenting by plenty of oral practice. If the problem arises when they have to choose the appropriate letters, make sure they put down a letter as each sound is segmented, rather than trying to do them all at once. When they have done this, ask them to sound and blend the letters they have selected. At this point, they may notice missing letters or find some letters to be in the wrong order. This approach is, of course, what we recommend be done in class as well, but working one-to-one with slower learners outside the lesson will help them focus on hearing the sounds in the word.

Group testing of phonic skills

The tests described so far are all designed for individual administration. However, we have found it useful to devise tests of spelling (with a reading element) for the busy class teacher to use (*Phonics Bug*, Watson and Johnston, 2010). These tests can be given to the whole class, as a screening to see which children are making slow progress. The results will help you decide which children need to do the individual nonword reading tests. The children read sentences like:

The dog ran into the ____ (road rode)

The children get these sentences on printed sheets and circle the correct words. Children can work through them in their own time as a class assessment, or the tests can be administered individually, with you reading the sentence frame if need be and the child deciding which is the correct spelling of the word to complete the sentence.

Making a record of children's difficulties

When children read the nonwords in Appendix 7, or the words and nonwords in the Hull Diagnostic Phonics Checks (Appendix 6), their errors can be identified and marked off on the catch-up sheets we have provided in Appendix 8. These sheets will not only guide you as to what revisiting to do with each child, but you may also find that there are groups of children with similar needs who can be put together for catch-up work. These are not exhaustive tests of everything that the child has been taught, but they can give you a snapshot of the kinds of difficulties that they are having.

A case study

We used many of these approaches to understand the reading problems of a boy with special educational needs. A fuller description of this case study is given in Johnston and Watson (2005). Anthony started school a year later than his classmates, as he was not ready for school, both socially and emotionally, and because he had poor receptive and expressive language. He also had hearing difficulties which affected his speech. He was 5.9 years old when he started school, and he was allocated a Supervisory Assistant to support his learning. His class took part in our study in Clackmannanshire, which carried out the analytic phonics plus phonological awareness training programme for two terms (see Chapter 1). This means his class was learning about letter sounds in the initial position of words (as is typical in analytic phonics in the UK) for 10 minutes a day for 16 weeks, and he also had 10 minutes a day analysing and synthesising sounds in spoken words.

Before the programme started, we tested him on the British Picture Vocabulary Test (Dunn *et al.*, 1982), on which he scored 54 (where the average is 100). This is a test of receptive vocabulary. The child sees a page with four pictures on it, the tester says the name of one of them, e.g. 'cup', and the child has to choose the picture to go with the spoken word. The other children in this group scored an average of 90.2, therefore it was clear that this boy was very much below average in vocabulary knowledge. We gave him the BAS Word Reading Test (Elliott *et al.*, 1977), and the Schonell Spelling test (Schonell and Schonell, 1952); he got no scores on these tests, but neither did the other children in this group. He did know a few letter names, but fewer than the others in his group, and he knew no letter sounds. We found he could not say any of the sounds in spoken words (e.g. what are the sounds in 'zoo'?), and he could not provide any rhymes (e.g. what rhymes with 'hop'?). However, many other children in the study also started out with no reading, spelling, letter knowledge, phoneme segmentation or rhyme ability.

REFLECTIVE TASK

Anthony started school with delayed language development and hearing difficulties, and his vocabulary knowledge was well below the average for his age.

What are your expectations for his progress in a) word reading, b) spelling, and c) reading comprehension?

The analytic phonics plus phonological awareness group Anthony was in learnt 16 letter sounds by March of the first year at school. The other children knew most of them when we did our tests in March, and Anthony knew 11 of them. However, he still could not segment phonemes in spoken words, or give rhyming words, although the other children in the group got about a third of the answers right on these two tests. The other children were reading and spelling around the right level for their age, but Anthony was still not scoring on these tests.

At this point, Anthony and his group started on the synthetic phonics programme. However, in November of Anthony's second year at school, an Individual Educational Programme was devised for him. A particular focus of this programme was his delayed language development. He was taught by a speech therapist and a learning support teacher to help improve his articulation, oral communication, listening and attention skills, and also his understanding of spatial concepts and grammatical structures. There was also work on his sound blending, visual memory, visual discrimination and visual closure, and motor co-ordination skills. We tested Anthony and the rest of the group's reading and spelling again in May of the second year at school. The children in this group were now reading 11 months ahead of age, and spelling around 8.5 months ahead of age (mean chronological age was 7.8 years). Anthony had made progress too, he got a score of 5.5 years on the word reading test (at the age of 8.8 years), but did not get a spelling score.

In January of his fourth year at school, he gained a word reading score of 6.8 years, and a spelling age of 7.0 years (when he was aged 9.6 years). He scored 100% on the letter sounds, phoneme segmentation, and CVC nonword reading tests (his group as a whole scored 87% on the letter-sound test, 66.7% on the phoneme-segmentation test, and 87% on the nonword test!). By analysing his reading errors, we found that he was able to use a phonic approach to reading, as the excellent nonword reading score suggests, but he still had some problems with blending. For example, he sounded out /sp/ /or/ /t/ but could not blend the sounds to pronounce the words. We could also see he was using a phonic approach to spelling, for example, writing 'yeer' for 'year'. A test carried out in March of his fifth year at school showed that he read correctly 91.6% of nonwords with initial consonant blends (e.g. 'glat'), 100% of nonwords with final consonant blends (e.g. 'kust'), 100% of nonwords with vowel digraphs (e.g. 'naik'), and 75% of nonwords with silent 'e's (e.g. 'bime'). His word reading and spelling was now at the 9-year-old level (at the age of 10.3 years). He had worked out for himself that blending at the syllable level was a good strategy with multi-syllabic words, but he had problems such as not knowing where to use 'c' or 'k' in spelling, or whether 'c' had a soft or hard sound in reading.

He had a very good teacher supporting his learning who carried out her own programme with him, which was similar to a revisiting programme we had offered to schools at that time. She noted that Anthony succeeded in tasks where he followed the systematic, defined procedure used in synthetic phonics, that is, sounding and blending for reading, and segmenting spoken words for spelling. In his sixth year at school, she concentrated on helping him read words with two and three syllables. The procedure was to identify syllables, sound and blend the letters within the syllables, and then blend the syllables together. For spelling, he practised learning to break up words into syllables, spelling each syllable, and then blending the syllables together to check he had the right letters. He also learnt spelling rules and was also encouraged to examine whether his spelling 'looked right'; if it did not, he was encouraged to try another digraph having the same sound. Together with the assistance of an occupational therapist, his Support for Learning teacher helped Anthony strengthen his hand-writing skills, but he was also taught to touch type to help him work faster and more efficiently.

Anthony also had a lot of help with his reading comprehension, but when he was 10.6 years old, he was understanding what he read only at a 6.9-year-old level. There was no evidence of his word reading being slow and effortful as on a test of how many words he could read in a minute his performance was average (Nicolson and Fawcett, 1998), so this is an unlikely explanation of his poor reading comprehension. We did not assess his listening skills, but given his language problems it is very likely that they were below the average for his age; that is, it is likely that he would have shown poor comprehension of spoken sentences. His Support for Learning teacher devised a series of progressive procedures for comprehension that Anthony could follow to help him read with understanding, based on the fact that he did well when he had clear procedures to follow. She worked on getting him to identify a sentence in a piece of text, highlight key word(s), read the key word, read around the key word, return to the beginning of the sentence and read it again. She then asked him questions about the meaning of the sentence. However, even at the end of his seventh year at school he was still only showing reading comprehension at the 7.1-year-old level. Table 8.2 charts Anthony's progress from the third to the seventh year at school. Did you predict this pattern of performance when you did the reflective task?

Table 8.2 Anthony's reading and spelling at the end of the third, fifth and seventh years at school

	Third year at school	Fifth year at school	Seventh year at school
Chronological age	8.8	10.6	12.6
Word reading age	5.5	9.2	12.4
Spelling age	0.0	8.9	11.2
Reading comprehension	–	6.9	7.1

Anthony made excellent progress in word reading and spelling. Given that by the seventh year at school his classmates were on average aged 11.6 years, his performance in word reading and spelling was very creditable indeed, as he had worked his way up to the level of performance that was expected for his age. However, his reading comprehension was still well below the average for his age; his score of 7.1 years can be converted into a standard score of 72 (where the average is 100). On a test of vocabulary knowledge taken at the end of his sixth year at school, he only gained a standard score of 63 (up from 54 when he started school). Vocabulary knowledge is more closely associated with reading comprehension than word reading and spelling, so despite Anthony's excellent progress in word reading and spelling, his impaired language skills were an impediment to him developing good reading comprehension. However, despite his low ability, the synthetic phonics approach, together with considerable learning support, helped him develop word reading and spelling skills appropriate for his age. There is a view that we have often heard expressed that children with special educational needs cannot learn by a phonics approach. We have shown that this not need be the case, and that persisting with the synthetic phonics method and giving appropriate learning support can lead to an excellent outcome.

Impact of Phonics Check in England: A case study

In the section 'The Phonics Screening Check' above, we showed that between 2012 and 2013 11% more children reached the expected level on the Phonics Check. Here we present some data from a school in a 'leafy suburb' in England where *Letters and Sounds* (DfES, 2007) is used for teaching phonics. In such an area it would be expected that children would be reading above the average, as the test we used was standardised on a sample that included children from disadvantaged as well as advantaged areas. Although *Letters and Sounds* eschews the use of non-phonic cues for reading, children in this class were encouraged to use them when dealing with unfamiliar words in text.

We are fortunate enough to have word-reading scores from a class in this school at the end of Reception in 2012. It can be seen that 25% of these children failed to gain a score on the British Ability Scales Word Reading Test (Elliott *et al.*, 1977), and around half of the class did not meet the expected level in the Phonics Check when they sat it in 2013. We also have data from a Reception class in the same school in 2014, with the same teacher in charge. It can be seen that only 6.7% of her pupils failed to gain a score on the test of word reading, which means that 18.3% more pupils had made a start on reading independently than in 2012. Furthermore, the children's reading scores in 2014 were 1.25 years above age level, whereas in 2012, they were only .63 years above age level.

Table 8.3 Comparison of performance of two Reception classes in England before and after the introduction of the Phonics Check

	Age (years)	Reading age (years)	Reading age above age level (years)	% of non-readers
Reception 2011–12, N = 28	5.21	5.83	0.63	25.00
Reception 2013–14, N = 30	5.25	6.50	1.25	6.70

It seems likely that the pace of phonics teaching had increased between 2012 and 2014 due to information being available on the level of performance expected on the Phonics Check. These figures might show a further improvement if children were no longer given contradictory information about the approach to take when tackling unfamiliar words. It is also possible that an increased amount of catch-up work, along the lines that Anthony received, would lead to fewer children failing to score on a reading test at the end of Reception. If much of the groundwork for good performance in the Phonics Check can be covered in Reception by teaching Phases 2 to 4, this would allow Year 1 teachers sufficient time to work with all pupils on the Phase 5 skills tested in Section 2 of the Phonics Check.

A SUMMARY OF **KEY POINTS**

➤ The government Phonics Check in England provides an indication of how well children in a class are doing with phonics, compared to the level expected at the end of Year 1; it can also provide some information on what catch-up work individual children need to do.

➤ Diagnostic tests of phonic skill can be carried out to pinpoint slow learners' areas of difficulty.

➤ These diagnostic phonics tests can be used to develop individually devised learning support programmes.

➤ We have shown that even a child with marked language problems was able to read words and spell well using the synthetic phonics approach, and a considerable amount of learning support tailored to his needs.

➤ We have outlined a case study where children in Reception classes in a school in England had better reading scores after feedback from the school's Phonics Check performance in 2012.

REFERENCES REFERENCES **REFERENCES** REFERENCES REFERENCES REFERENCES

DfE (2013a) *The phonics screening check: responding to the results*. London: DfE. https://www.gov.uk/government/uploads/system/uploads/attachment_data/file/285349/The_phonics_screening_check_responding_to_the_results--.pdf (retrieved 27 August 2014).

DfE (2013b) *Phonics Screening Check and National Curriculum Assessments at Key Stage 1 in England: 2013*. London: DfE. https://www.gov.uk/government/publications/phonics-screening-check-and-national-curriculum-assessments-at-key-stage-1-in-england-2013 (retrieved 27 August 2014).

DfES (2007) *Letters and Sounds*. London: DfES. http://www.standards.dfes.gov.uk/local/clld/las.html (retrieved 27 August 2014).

Dunn, L.M., Dunn, L.M., Whetton, C. and Pintillie, D. (1982) *British Picture Vocabulary Scale*. Windsor: NFER Nelson.

Elliott, C.D., Murray, D.J. and Pearson, L.S. (1977) *The British Abilities Scale*. Windsor: NFER Nelson.

Johnston, R.S., Walker, J., Howatson, K. and Stockburn, A. (in preparation) What kinds of difficulties do slower learners experience in the Phonics Check?

Johnston, R.S. and Watson, J. (2005) *The effects of synthetic phonics teaching on reading and spelling attainment, a seven year longitudinal study*. Edinburgh: Scottish Executive Education Department. http://www.scotland.gov.uk/library5/education/sptrs-00.asp (retrieved 27 August 2014).

Nicolson, R. and Fawcett, A. (1998) *One Minute Reading Test, in Dyslexia Early Screening Test*. Oxford: Harcourt.

Schonell, F.J. and Schonell, F.E. (1952) *Diagnostic and attainment testing* (2nd edition). Edinburgh: Oliver & Boyd.

Standards and Testing Agency (2012) *Phonics Screening Check*. London: DfE. http://media.education. gov.uk/assets/files/pdf/p/phonics%20screening%20check%20sample%20materials.pdf (retrieved 27 August 2014).

Watson, J.E. and Johnston, R.S. (2010) *Phonics Bug*. Harlow: Pearson.

9

Letters and Sounds, *Phonics Bug* and *Read Write Inc*: selecting a programme to prepare children for the Phonics Check

Learning objectives

In this chapter you will:

- learn about what needs to be included in a synthetic phonics scheme to fit the requirements of the National Curriculum;
- see examples of the words that are covered for reading and spelling in Phases 2 to 5 of *Letters and Sounds*;
- see how two commercial programmes, *Phonics Bug* and *Read Write Inc*, are structured.

TEACHERS' STANDARDS

3. Demonstrate good subject and curriculum knowledge
4. Plan and teach well structured lessons
5. Adapt teaching to respond to the strengths and needs of all pupils
6. Make accurate and productive use of assessment

This chapter looks in detail at *Letters and Sounds* (DfES, 2007), *Phonics Bug* (Watson and Johnston, 2010) and *Read Write Inc* (Miskin, 2011) from the perspective of preparing children for England's Phonics Check at the end of Year 1.

In Table 9.1, we show some guidelines for teaching a synthetic phonics programme. In the first column is a summary of the guidance issued by the Teaching and Development Agency (TDA, 2011) to initial teacher-training providers on how phonics should be taught. It shows very clearly the progression that synthetic phonics teaching should follow, but it is not explicit about how common exception (irregular/tricky words) should be taught for reading and spelling. To clarify this, in the second column we have shown the up-to-date statutory requirements and guidance given in the National Curriculum (DfE, 2013).

Letters and Sounds

A recent study by NFER (Walker *et al.*, 2013) shows that *Letters and Sounds* (DfES, 2007) is still the most widely used synthetic phonics programme in England. However, it also shows that other strategies for decoding words are still being taught alongside the phonics approach in schools, such as sight word teaching and encouraging children to guess words from picture cues and context. These approaches are explicitly ruled out in the National Curriculum (DfE, 2013) and in *Letters and Sounds* itself; children will develop

Table 9.1 Teaching and Development Agency Guidelines (TDA, 2011) and National Curriculum (DfE, 2013) Statutory Requirements

Teaching and Development Agency guidelines	National Curriculum Statutory Requirements and Guidance (revision of Reception and teaching from Year 1 onwards)
Grapheme to phoneme correspondences (GPCs) to be introduced at the rate of about three to five a week, starting with single letters and a sound for each, then going on to the sounds represented by digraphs (e.g. *sh* and *oo*) and larger grapheme units (e.g. *air*, *igh*, *eigh*).	Pupils should understand 'that the letter(s) on the page represent the sounds in spoken words' and this 'should underpin pupils' reading and spelling of all words' (p19).
Blending of phonemes for reading, starting after the first few GPCs have been taught and then working with more GPCs as they are taught.	Pupils should be taught 'to read accurately by blending sounds in unfamiliar words containing GPCs that have been taught' (p20).
Segmenting of words into phonemes for spelling, starting after the first few GPCs have been taught and then working with more GPCs as they are taught.	Spelling should be taught by 'segmenting spoken words into sounds before choosing graphemes to represent the sounds' (p50).
Introduction of the most common spellings for sounds first, and then introducing alternative sounds for spellings and alternative spellings for sounds.	Pupils should be taught to 'respond speedily with the correct sound to graphemes (letters or groups of letters) for all 40+ phonemes, including, where applicable, alternative sounds for graphemes' (p20).
Introduction of strategies for reading and spelling common, high frequency, words containing unusual GPCs.	Reading: Pupils should be taught to 'read common exception words, noting unusual correspondences between spelling and sound and where these occur in the word' (p20). Spelling: 'Pupils' attention should be drawn to the grapheme–phoneme correspondences that do and do not fit in with what has been taught so far' (p54).
Provision of opportunities for the application of word-reading skills in reading books which are closely matched to children's developing skills (level-appropriate decodable texts) to support them in using their phonemic strategies as a first approach to reading and spelling and to experiencing success.	Pupils should be taught to 'read aloud accurately books that are consistent with their developing phonic knowledge and that do not require them to use other strategies to work out words' (p20).

sight word recognition after a few readings of an unfamiliar word via a phonics approach. This programme is still available online, but it is no longer in print. *Letters and Sounds* gives a very clear outline of how to teach synthetic phonics, but teachers have had to do a considerable amount of work to develop the actual lessons. In Chapters 6 and 7 we looked in detail at how phonics lessons are taught in Phases 2 to 6 of the programme, and in Chapter 8 we outlined the guidance that the Standards and Testing Agency (2012) has published on what can be included in the Phonics Check. To summarise here what may be included: children may be tested on all of the single letters, and on adjacent consonants, consonant digraphs (ch, ck, ff, ll, ng, sh, ss, th, zz, ph, wh), vowel digraphs (ar, ee, oi, oo,

Table 9.2 Letters and Sounds Phases 2 and 3

Phase 2: Set 1 letters				Set 2 letters				Set 3 letters				Set 4 letters			
s	a	t	p	i	n	m	d	g	o	c	k	ck	e	u	r
			at, sat pat tap	it is sit sat	an in nip	am man mam	Dad sad	tag gag	got on not pot	can cot cop	kid kit Kim	kick sock sack dock	get pet ten net	up mum run mug	rim rip ram rat rag rug
							and*		_got_ _on_ _not_	_can_	_to**_		_get_	_up_ _mum_ **the** **no** **go**	_rim_

Set 5 letters					Phase 3: Set 6 letters			Set 7 letters				New graphemes			
h	b	f ff	l ll	ss	j	v	w	x	y	z zz	qu	ch	sh	th	ng
had him his hot hut	but big back	of, if, off fit fin fun, fig	lap let leg lot lit, bell	ass less hiss mass	jam jacket	van vat	will win	mix vixen	yap yes	zip Zak	quiz quit	chop chin	ship shop	them then	ring rang
had	_but_	_of_ _if_ _off_	**I** _into_					**me** **be**			**he** **my** **by**			_them_ _then_ _that_ _this_ _with_	**they** **she**

New graphemes

ai	ee	igh	oa	long oo	short oo	ar	or	ur	ow	oi	ear	air	ure	er
wait Gail hail pain	see feel weep	high sigh	coat load	too zoo boot hoof	look foot cook	bar car bark	for fork cord cork	fur burn urn burp	now down owl towel	oil boil coin coil	ear dear fear hear	air fair hair lair	sure lure	hammer letter
				too	_look_ **we** **are**		_for_		_now_ _down_	**you** **her**				**all** **was**

*High frequency words appear in italics.
**Tricky words appear in bold.

or, a-e, ai, au, aw, ay, ea, e-e, ew, i-e, ie, ir, oa, o-e, ou, ow, oy, ue, u-e, ur), vowel trigraphs (air, igh), and two-syllable words. This means that children need to be taught Phases 2 to 5 in order to cover the phonics that can be included in the Phonics Check.

In order to get an impression of what sorts of words need to be taught, Tables 9.2, 9.3 and 9.4 show examples of the words suggested for use in Phases 2 to 5 of *Letters and Sounds*. We have put in some sample decodable words, and all of the common exception (tricky words) (to be taught as partially decodable words). There is a fuller version of these tables in Appendix 9, which lists all of the words suggested for teaching reading and spelling in these phases in the *Letters and Sounds* programme. It can be seen that Phase 2 covers one-syllable CVC words, without vowel digraphs, using the first 19 letters of the

Table 9.3 *Letters and Sounds* Phase 4

CVCC words						
Words using sets 1–7 letters			**Words using Phase 3 graphemes**		**Polysyllabic words**	
went*	best	fond	champ	shift	*children*	shampoo
it's	tilt	gust	chest	shelf	helpdesk	Chester
help	lift	ask***	tenth	joint	sandpit	giftbox
just	lost	fast***	theft	boost	windmill	shelter
went, it's help just					*children*	**said**** **have like, so do, some, come, were there, little one, when out, what**
CCV and CCVC words						
Words using sets 1–7 letters		**Words using Phase 3 phonemes**				
from	grip	green	flair	clear	speech	
stop	glad	fresh	trail	train	thrill	
spot	glass***	steep	cream	swing	treetop	
frog	grass***	tree	clown	droop	starlight	
CVCC, CCCVC and CCCVCC words						
Words using sets 1–7 letters			**Words using Phase 3 graphemes**	**Polysyllabic words**		
stand	crust	graft***	crunch	driftwood		
crisp	tramp	grant***	drench	twisting		
trend	grunt	blast***	trench	printer		
trust	crept		Grinch			

* High frequency words appear in italics.
** Tricky words appear in bold.
*** In the North of England, where the letter a is pronounced /a/, these are appropriate as Phase 4 words.

Table 9.4 Letters and Sounds Phase 5

New graphemes for reading

ay	ou	ie	ea	oy	ir	ue	ue	ey
*day**	*out*	pie	sea	boy	girl	clue	cue	money
play	*about*	lie	seat	toy	sir	blue	due	honey
may	cloud, scout	tie	bead	joy	bird	glue	hue	donkey
say		die	read	oyster	shirt	true	venue	cockney

aw	wh	wh	ph	ew	ew	oe	au
saw	*when*	*who*	Philip	blew	stew	toe	Paul
paw	*what*	*whose*	Philippa	chew	few	hoe	haul
raw	*which*	*whole*	phonics	grew	new	doe	daub
claw	*where*	*whom*	sphinx	drew	dew	foe	launch

a-e	e-e	i-e	o-e	u-e	u-e
came	*these*	*like*	bone	June	huge
made	*Pete*	*time*	pole	flute	cube
make	*Eve*	*pine*	home	prune	tube
take	*Steve*	*ripe*	alone	rude	use

Alternative pronunciations of known graphemes for reading

a	a	a	e	e	i	i
hat	*fast***	*was*	bed	*he*	tin	*mind*
	*path***	*what*		*me*		*find*
	*pass***	*wash*		*recent, region*		*wild*
	*father***	*wasp*				*pint*

o	o	u	u	u	ow	ow	ie	ie
hot	*no*	but	*put***	*unit*	down	*low*	pie	chief
	so		*pull***	*union*		*grow*		brief
	gold		*push***	*unicorn*		*snow*		field
	cold		*fall***	*music*		*glow*		shield

(Continued)

Table 9.4 (Continued)

ea			
sea	head, dead, deaf, ready	farmer	

er			
her, fern, stern, Gerda	out		

ou			
you, soup, group	*could*, would, should	mould, shoulder, boulder	

c			
cat	cell, central, acid, cycle		

ch			
chin	school, Christmas, chemist, cord	chef, Charlene, machine, brochure	

y			
yes	gym, crystal, mystery, pyramid	*by, my, try, why*	*very*, happy, funny, carry

ey		
money	*they*, grey, obey, pray	

g		
got	gent, gym, gem, Gill	

Alternative spellings for phonemes

/**ch**/: picture, catch. /**j**/: fudge, hedge. /**m**/: lamb, limb. /**n**/: gnat, knit. /**r**/: wrap, wren. /**s**/: listen, house. /**z**/: please, tease. /**u**/: *some*, none. /**i**/: happy, donkey. /**ear**/: *here*, beer. /**ar**/: father, half. /**air**/: where, pear, bare. /**or**/: all, four, caught. /**ur**/: learn, word. /**oo**/: would, pull. /**ai**/: play, take. /**ee**/: sea, these, happy, chief, key. /**igh**/: pie, *by, like*. /**oa**/: low, toe, bone. /(**y**) **oo**/: cue, tune, stew. /**oo**/: clue, tune, June, blew. /**sh**/: special, station, sure, chef.

New phoneme /**zh**/: treasure, visual, beige

*High frequency words appear in italics.
**South of England only.

alphabet; Phase 3 introduces the rest of the alphabet, plus some consonant digraphs, vowel digraphs and two-syllable words; Phase 4 covers adjacent consonants; and Phase 5 covers new graphemes for reading, alternative pronunciations of known graphemes for reading, alternative spellings of phonemes and phonic rules such as the pronunciation of 'c' and 'g' before 'e', 'i' and 'y'.

Review of two commercial programmes: *Phonics Bug* and *Read Write Inc*

Having outlined the progression in *Letters and Sounds* (DfES, 2007) up to the end of Phase 5, which covers the teaching needed for the Phonics Screening Check, this chapter will now review two commercial programmes that schools can buy to implement synthetic phonics teaching according to the method outlined in the National Curriculum (DfE, 2013). Two popular programmes are *Read Write Inc* (Miskin, 2011) and *Phonics Bug* (Watson and Johnston, 2010, formerly *Fast Phonics First*). These two programmes provide the coverage needed for the Phonics Check, as outlined by the Standards and Testing Agency (2012), and they also fit with the statutory requirements of the National Curriculum. They provide much more guidance on the content of daily lessons than *Letters and Sounds*. There are commercial materials available providing daily lessons for *Letters and Sounds*, but some of them also recommend the sight word teaching of high frequency and common exception (tricky) words, which is contrary to the statutory requirements in the National Curriculum, and to the method outlined in *Letters and Sounds*.

Phonics Bug

Phonics Bug (Watson and Johnston, 2010) comes from the programme used in the Clackmannanshire Study, and *Letters and Sounds* was developed in very close alignment with it, which means that the lesson structures are very similar. It is organised according to the Phonics Phases, as outlined in Tables 9.2, 9.3 and 9.4.

Structure

There are two *Phonics Bug Teaching and Assessment Guides*, one for Reception (Primary 1 in Scotland) and one for Key Stage 1 (Primaries 2 and 3) (Watson and Johnston, 2010). The Reception Guide covers Phases 2 to 4 (Section 1 of the Phonics Check, see Tables 9.2 and 9.3), and the Key Stage 1 Guide covers Phases 5 and 6 (Phase 5 covers Section 2 of the Phonics Check, see Table 9.4). The daily lessons contained in these guides can be taught either by using a large magnetic board and plastic letters, or by using online software on an interactive whiteboard, helped along by an animated speaking 'bug' character, which the children can name; we call him Timmo. There are demonstration videos available online which show how to use the software to teach all aspects of the lessons. These can be found under the Getting Started menu on the Bug Club Buzz website (http://bugclubnews.pearson.com/).

The lesson structure is the same for the whole programme from Phase 2 to the end of Phase 6. The Guides contain fully specified lesson plans for each day, showing all the words needed for teaching reading and spelling. There are photocopiable worksheets for each lesson, and there are online phonics games and decodable books suitable for use after each set of letters has been taught.

Getting started with *Phonics Bug*: learning a few letter–sound correspondences

Initially, soon after starting school, children are taught the letter sounds s, a, t, p, on a whole class basis, taking one day to learn each letter. If the teacher is using the online software, there are animated cartoons for each of the letters, showing what sounds they represent and how they are written. For example, the first sound taught is for the letter 's'; this is shown as a snake making a 'ssss' sound and there is also a demonstration of how to form the letter. In order to develop their phoneme awareness skills the children see videos of a little girl in a sailor suit, a seesaw, a possum, a dinosaur, and a sunset; the children try to work out what the word is, and then the TV presenter tells them what it is.

The children then see a set of words containing the letter 's' in order to develop their visual discrimination. Without reading the words, a child in turn highlights the 's' in each word on the board, saying whether it is at the beginning, the middle or the end of the word. From the small set of letters they have on their individual magnetic boards, the children find the letter 's' and feel the shape of it. The teacher (or the online software) then demonstrates how to form the letter 's'; the children skywrite the letter in the air, and then a child directs the teacher on how to form the letter as she or he writes it on the magnetic board or on the empty work area on the interactive whiteboard.

Starting to sound and blend for reading, and to segment for spelling, using 's, a, t, p'

After four lessons, when the children have learnt the letter sounds 's, a, t, p', they start to sound and blend for reading and to segment for spelling using words made up from the taught letters, e.g. 'tap, pat, sat'. Firstly, the previously taught letter sounds are revised at the start of each session, and then the children watch either the teacher or the software programme put up the letters for the word 'tap'. These letters are spaced out, the sound for each one is given in sequence, and they are blended by the teacher or by Timmo, the letters being moved together from left to right to indicate the blending process. Then the letters are spaced out again and a child comes to the board to do the blending, smoothly co-articulating the sounds and pushing the magnetic letters together, while the whole class blends along with them. The full set of words used for reading in this lesson is 'tap, pat, sat, as, at, sap', and the last two words are blended by the children without the help of the teacher or Timmo.

Then the children hear the word 'pats' and spell it using the following procedure. They hear the word and repeat it, then they spell it using a small set of magnetic letters on their individual magnetic boards. The first time they say the word they identify the phoneme /p/ and put down the letter 'p' on the left-hand side of their boards. Then they say the word again, identify the /a/ phoneme and put down the letter 'a' beside the 'p', and so on until all of the sounds of the word have been represented by a letter in sequence. A child then comes to the board and spells 'pats'; the rest of the class checks if they got it right by sounding and blending it. After that the word 'taps' is spoken for spelling, and then the word 'tap' is spelt after the children have seen and named a picture of a tap.

Learning the new letter 'i'

The lesson structure used for the entire programme starts at this point. The children revise the letters 's, a, t, p', and read the words 'as, tap, pat, sat', write the letters 's, a, t, p', and spell the words 'at, sap' (the words used for the revision of reading in this lesson were used for spelling the previous day, and vice versa). The children now learn the new letter sound 'i', seeing the animated video for that sound. After that the children visually search for the new letter in some words on the board (without reading them). For reading, they see the word 'it' on the board and sound and blend to find out its pronunciation, doing the same in turn with the words 'pip, pit, sip, tip, tips'.

For spelling, they hear the word 'is', say the first sound /i/, and select the letter 'i' from a small selection of letters on their individual magnetic boards. The children say the word again, say the next sound /s/, and then find the letter 's' for that sound and place it to the right of the letter 'i'. Next a child spells the word on the board, and the class sounds and blends the word to make sure they have the letters in the right order. Then they hear 'sips' and spell it using the same procedure, and finally they see a picture representing 'sit' and they say and spell it.

The children practise skywriting the new letter 'i' and a child guides the teacher on how to write the letter on the board. There are also worksheets so that the children can practise writing the letters with a pencil. Spelling is emphasised right from the start in this programme, as it is a very good way of learning phoneme awareness. At this stage the children do not spell words that they have just read, otherwise they may not be spelling independently.

The number of words read and spelt daily increases each day until Unit 4; from this point there are four words for reading revision and four words for spelling revision every day, plus eight new words for reading and four new words for spelling using the newly taught letter sound. These daily letter–sound (or grapheme to phoneme correspondence) sessions continue throughout the programme. Every few days a language session introduces common exception words and connected text for reading and spelling.

Language sessions

After eight letter–sound learning sessions, the children start the Language sessions, where they are introduced to connected text by reading and spelling captions and sentences, and they learn to read and spell common exception/irregular/tricky words. These sessions occur after every four or five new phoneme lessons. If using the online resources, phonics games can now be played to reinforce the learning.

There are *Phonics Bug* decodable story books that can be used as each language session is reached. For example, the first Language session introduces four decodable books that use the letters 's, a, t, p, i, n, m, d', e.g. 'Sid Did It'. Where appropriate, these books also contain the taught common exception (tricky) words.

Table 9.5 shows a complete lesson from Phase 3, and its associated language session.

Teaching common exception/'tricky' words

After 14 lessons, the children start to learn tricky words in the Language session, that is words which are either common exception words (called irregular words in this scheme), or words which go beyond the phonics being taught at that stage. Teaching these words allows the children to make a very early start on story books. The procedure for teaching high frequency and common exception/tricky/irregular words is explained on page 5 of the *Reception Teaching and Assessment Guide* (Watson and Johnston, 2010): 'Phonics Bug approaches "irregular" words with the premise that almost all words can be phonically decoded to some extent. Children are encouraged to use their phonic knowledge to

Table 9.5 Lesson for the Phase 3 vowel digraph ee, and related language session

Revision	The children revise the previously taught graphemes: y, zz, qu, ch, sh, th, ng, ai.
	They read: rain, tail, nail, snail (used for spelling the day before).
	They write and spell: sh, th, ng, ai; sail, wait, main, train (used for reading the day before).
Lesson	New grapheme 'ee' is introduced in animated video.
	Visual search. The children search for this new grapheme in printed words: eel, teeth, bee, sheep. They say whether it comes in the initial, middle or final position of words, reinforcing a left-to-right visual search strategy.
	Using the new grapheme, together with previously taught ones, the children sound and blend printed words for reading: eel, teeth, seem, sheep, peel, tree, see, sleep.
	Using the new grapheme they spell, using magnetic letters on their own individual boards, the words: green, feet, sheep, bee. They can additionally see videos for: seed, tree.
	They write the new grapheme 'ee', by feeling the shapes of the magnetic letters, skywriting the letters in the air, and directing the teacher how to write the letters on the board.
	The children can now play online games for the previous unit, practise writing the letters on the worksheet, and read decodable *Phonics Bug* books for the previously taught graphemes: ch, sh, th, ng.
Language session	After a block of new graphemes has been taught, including 'ee', the children learn the common exception words 'we' and 'are', their attention being drawn to the less decodable parts. They read or write captions and sentences using the common exception words and words made up from the taught graphemes.
	They read: Can we go to the zoo?, Yes, we are free this week.
-	They spell on the interactive whiteboard: footstool, aim high, A bee by the tree.
Follow-up	They write: footstool, aim high, A bee by the tree. Get the children to talk about the picture of a boat.

help them decode a word as far as they can, while you can point out and talk through the irregular aspect to help them to read the word'.

Here are some examples of the teaching of tricky words, drawing attention to the decodable and not so decodable parts of the word. When the children are taught how to read the word 'to' in Phase 2 it is explained to them that the letter 'o' sounds /oo/ in this case. Having introduced the word for reading, children then spell the word in sentence context. When the word 'are' is introduced for spelling in Phase 3, the teacher explains that the 'e' is silent but is needed for spelling. In Phase 4, the teacher explains that in the word 'said', the 'ai' sounds as /e/; in the word 'have', the 'e' is not pronounced but is needed for spelling; in 'so' the 'o' sounds like its letter name and is pronounced /oa/. The word 'like' is also introduced at this point; this is phonically regular but as silent letters are not introduced until Phase 5 the children are told that the 'i' sounds like its letter name, and that the 'e' is not pronounced and is needed for spelling.

Pace
Phases 2 to 4: Reception
According to *Letters and Sounds* (DfES, 2007), it is envisaged that Phases 2 to 4 inclusive will be taught in Reception; this gives complete coverage of Section 1 of the Phonics

Check. In *Phonics Bug* there are 65 grapheme/language sessions to cover these phases. A steady and manageable pace would be to teach 24 lessons up to the end of Unit 4 (Phase 2) in the Autumn term; see Table 9.6. This means that by Christmas the children will also have learnt some common exception words, and will have moved from reading captions and sentences to reading decodable books (containing some taught common exception/tricky words). In the Spring term, the children can be taught in 20 lessons up to the end of Unit 8, Phase 3. This would leave 21 lessons to be taught in the Summer term, taking children up to the end of Unit 12, Phase 4.

This is a slower pace than in the Clackmannanshire Study, where Phases 2 to 4 were covered in 16 weeks, and were completed by Easter of Primary 1 (Reception). It is of interest therefore that even with this faster pace we found that all of this teaching could be done very effectively on a whole class basis, in schools in areas of moderate to severe deprivation. In our study the children were not divided up into ability groups and the whole class worked at the same pace; this continued in the second year of school.

Although there are assessments in this programme (see below), we did not find it necessary for children to reach complete mastery of what they had been taught before moving on. Take the example of a child who is having difficulty in learning the letter 'd', which comes at the end of Phase 2 when 19 letter sounds have been taught. If the child stays with the whole class programme, in the next lesson 'd' will be revised for reading, writing and spelling before the new letter sound for 'o' is taught. Furthermore, the words 'nod', 'dot' and 'dog' are used for reading and spelling words using the letter 'o', and these words will be revised the next day when the letter 'c' is taught. The new words for 'c' include the word 'cod', so 'd' comes up again. When 'k' is taught next, the word 'desk' is one of the words used. It can be seen that in a cumulative programme like this, the same letter sounds come up over and over again, which provides consolidation for slower learners. Because of this we have found that there is no need to hold back a group of children to do only Phase 2 level work, as Phase 3 work consolidates Phase 2 learning. If children continue for a long time in Phase 2 it will be a long time before they learn the final seven letters of the alphabet and so they will only be able to read a very limited range of texts. If necessary, slower learners can be given extra daily tuition outside the phonics lesson in order to keep up with their classmates, and guidance is given in the Guides on how to do this. We have found that staying in the whole class programme for phonics teaching spurs on slower learners; in one study we found that a special needs child, who was not thought to be capable of learning any phonics at all, learnt 23 letter sounds (she also found it be a lot of fun). Furthermore, we were told by a school inspector that the children's self esteem was better with whole class synthetic phonics teaching, and that there were fewer problems in the playground. However, the programme can also be used for teaching in ability groups, according to the teacher's professional judgement.

Phase 5: Year 1
Phase 5 work is largely concerned with teaching vowel digraphs, which is the greatest area of difficulty in the English spelling system for children. We have worked out a steady pace of teaching the phonics needed to do well in Section 2 of the Phonics Check (see Table 9.7), allowing a lot of days for consolidation and catch-up sessions, and days for worksheets, games and decodable readers.

As to the time it takes to teach a lesson, this varies a lot with the class and with the teacher's approach; it might take up to 40 to 45 minutes. A further 10 minutes can be spent on the worksheets, covering letter formation and visual discrimination of the letter; this work can be done later in the day.

Table 9.6 Phases 2 to 4 in *Phonics Bug*, and suggested teaching timetable

Phase	Unit	Focus	Common exception (irregular/tricky) words, keywords	Suggested teaching timetable
2	1	s a t p		Autumn term, Reception
2	2	i n m d		
2	3	g o c k	and, to	
2	4	ck e u	the, no, go	
2	5	h b f ff l ll ss	I, into	Spring term, Reception
3	6	j v w x	me, be	
3	7	y z zz qu	he, my, by	
3	8	ch sh th ng	they, she	
3	9	ai ee igh oa oo (long) oo (short)	we, are	Summer term, Reception
3	10	ar or ur ow oi	you, her	
3	11	ear air ure er	all, was	
4	12	Adjacent consonants (cvcc, ccvc, ccvcc, cccvc, cccvcc)	said, have, like, so, do, some, come, were, there, little, one, when, out, what	
			Teaching up to this point gives full coverage of Section 1 of the Phonics Check.	

Table 9.7 Phases 5 and 6 of *Phonics Bug*, and suggested teaching timetable

Phase	Unit	Focus	Common exception (irregular/tricky) words, key words	Suggested teaching timetable
5	13	zh wh ph	oh, their	Autumn term, Year 1
5	14	*long a*: ay a-e eigh/ey/ei	Mr, Mrs	
5	15	*long e*: ea e-e ie/ey/y	looked, called, asked	
5	16	*long i*: ie i-e y i	water, where	
5	17	*long o*: ow o-e o/oe	who, again	Spring term, Year 1
5	18	*long u*: ew ue u-e;	thought, through	
5	19	*short oo*: u/oul	work, laughed, because	
5	20	aw au al ir er ear	Thursday, Saturday, thirteen, thirty	
5	21	ou oy	different, any, many	Summer term, Year 1
5	22	ere/eer are/ear	eyes, friends	
5	23	c k ck ch	one, two, once	
5	24	ce/ci/cy sc/stl se	great, clothes	Autumn term, Year 2
5	25	ge/gi/gy dge	It's, I'm, I'll, I've	
5	26	le mb kn/gn wr	don't, can't, didn't	
5	27	tch sh ea (w)a	first, second, third	
6	28	suffix morphemes: ing ed	clearing, gleaming, rained, mailed	Spring term, Year 2
6	29	plural morphemes: s es	men, mice, feet, teeth, sheep	
6	30	prefix morphemes: re un prefix + root + suffix	vowel, consonant, prefix, suffix, syllable	

Assessment and grouping

There are seven assessments for Phases 2 to 4 (Reception), four assessments for Phase 5 (Year 1), and two assessments for Phase 6 (Year 2); see Table 9.8. Guidance is given in the Teaching Guides on how to interpret children's performance, and advice is given on helpful catch-up activities. The spelling assessments can be done as a whole class screening measure to save time, followed by individual reading assessments for the slower learners. From Phase 5 onwards we specify which units to re-teach for each item a child has difficulty with; these sessions largely deal with vowel digraphs, which are quite hard for all children to learn. These assessments can also be used to group children for teaching on the basis of their ability.

Table 9.8 *Phonics Bug* Assessments

Assessment	Areas covered	Phonics phases
Assessment sheet 1	Names and/or sounds of letters	Phases 2 and 3
Assessment sheet 2	Writing the letters of the alphabet	Phases 2 and 3
Assessment sheet 3	Sounds of vowel and consonant digraphs and trigraphs	Phase 3
Assessment sheet 4	Spellings of digraphs and trigraphs	Phase 3
Assessment sheet 5	Blending written nonwords for reading (CVC) Segmenting spoken nonwords for spelling (CVC)	Phase 3
Assessment sheet 6	Blending and segmenting CCVC, CVCC, and CCVCC nonwords	Phase 4
Assessment sheet 7	Writing about a picture Ticking the sentences that make sense	–
Additional assessment	Reading of taught common exception words (downloadable from the software)	Phase 3
Assessment sheet 8	Spelling of new graphemes and vowel digraphs/trigraphs	Phase 5, Units 13–21 of *Phonics Bug*
Assessment sheet 9	Spelling of new graphemes and vowel digraphs/trigraphs	Phase 5, Units 22–27 of *Phonics Bug*
Assessment sheet 10	Reading of new graphemes and vowel digraphs/trigraphs	Phase 5, Units 13–21 of *Phonics Bug*
Assessment sheet 11	Reading of new graphemes and vowel digraphs/trigraphs	Phase 5, Units 22–27 of *Phonics Bug*
Assessment sheet 12	Spelling: rules for adding suffixes and prefixes	Phase 6, Units 28–30 of *Phonics Bug*
Assessment sheet 13	Reading: rules for adding suffixes and prefixes	Phase 6, Units 28–30 of *Phonics Bug*

There is also a separate handbook, *Phonics Bug Prepare and Assess* (Betts, 2012), which gives further assessments to help prepare for the Phonics Check; this also has online games and online assessments.

Slower learners

There is more revision and consolidation in *Phonics Bug* lessons than in *Letters and Sounds* (DfES, 2007). This works very well with slower learners and the short discrete elements within the lessons help them to keep their concentration. The repetition of the same lesson structure every day is also helpful for them. The manipulation of magnetic letters is also very helpful, as they get tactile as well as visual and auditory information to enrich their learning of the letters. If the slower learners are kept with the rest of the class for their learning they are exposed to a rich array of printed words and are spurred on by seeing what other children are achieving. As this programme comes from the Clackmannanshire Study, we know that there are very few underachievers with this whole class teaching method. However, according to the teacher's professional judgement, the slower learners can be formed into a nurture group for extra consolidation work later in the day, and in the Guides we make some suggestions for work to help these children keep up with their classmates. We have found that the online phonic games go down well with these children, and indeed they are highly motivating for all of the children.

Parental support

We have produced a home-teaching CD, *My Fast Phonics Folder* (Johnston and Watson, 2012), which is completely compatible with the *Phonics Bug* teaching programme. This teaches Phase 2 to 4 phonics using an animated character; it also contains an alphabet song and interactive phonics games. A child can sit at the computer and work independently with the CD or carry out the activities with parental support. *My Fast Phonics Folder* also contains five colourful Activity Books covering Phases 2–5 for children to revisit what they have already covered in school and to reinforce new learning throughout the year.

Read Write Inc

Structure

The details of the programme are contained in the *Read Write Inc Phonics Handbook* (Miskin, 2011). The phonics teaching in *Read Write Inc* is organised into three sections: Speed Sounds Set 1, Speed Sounds Set 2, and Speed Sounds Set 3. There are daily lesson plans for all of the letter sounds that are taught. Table 9.9 shows in detail how Speed Sounds Set 1 is organised, and the letter sounds that are taught. As an overview, it can be said that after the first block of letter sounds have been taught, i.e. 'm, a, s, d, t', and the children have learnt to write them, the children read and spell words made up from the letters, i.e. 'mad, sad, dad, mat, sat, sam'. These words are then read and spelt daily as the next group of letter sounds are taught, i.e. ' i, n, p, g, o'. For example, on the day that 'i' is taught, the children read and spell 'mad, sad, dad, mat, sat, sam' again; when the letter 'o' is reached the children read and spell that word set for the last time. The words are read by blending, the letters being shown on Speed Cards or via magnetic letters. The words are spelt by breaking a spoken word down into its constituent phonemes and pressing a finger in sequence to represent each phoneme, this is called 'Fred' talk; when the children can do this they write down a few of the words. After the second group of letter sounds have been learnt, the next step is to blend and segment words and nonwords made up from the second group of letters; i.e. after 'o' has been taught the children read 'in, on, it, an, and, pin, got, dog, sit, tip, pan, gap, dig, top, ip, op, sop, gip, pog'. These items are then read and spelt every day while the new group of letter sounds are taught, i.e. 'c, k, u, b'. The blocks of letters 'f, e, l, h, sh', 'r, j, v, y, w' and 'th, z, ch, q, x, ng, nk' are taught in the same way, with the previous set of words being read and spelt as the new letter sounds are taught. A final set of 58 items are read and spelt at the end of the work on the Speed Sounds Set 1, covering adjacent consonants

Table 9.9 *Read Write Inc* Speed Sounds 1

Each day teach children one of these new speed sounds, write the letter, and Fred Talk words with the new sound:	Each day revise blending for reading and segmenting for spelling with these words:	At end of each block, introduce these new items for reading and spelling:
m a s d t	–	After 't' has been taught, teach blending for reading and segmenting for spelling with the words: mad, sad, dad, mat, sat, sam
i n p g o	Each day, after each new letter is taught children read and spell: mad, sad, dad, mat, sat, sam	After 'o' has been taught get the children to read and spell: in, on, it, an, and, pin, got, dog, sit, tip, pan, gap, dig, top, ip, op, sop, gip, pog
c k u b	Each day, after each new letter is taught children read and spell: in, on, it, an, and, pin, got, dog, sit, tip, pan, gap, dig, top, ip, op, sop, gip, pog	After 'b' has been taught, read and spell: bin, cat, cot, can, kit, mud, up, cup, bad, back, kick, lock, tog, bon, pim, bup
f e l h sh	Each day, after each new letter is taught children read and spell: bin, cat, cot, can, kit, mud, up, cup, bad, back, kick, lock, tog, bon, pim, bup	After 'sh' has been taught read and spell: met, set, fan, fun, fat, lip, log, let, had, hit, hen, ship, shop, fish, sack, gof, shup, hib, fot, gock
r j v y w	Each day, after each new letter is taught children read and spell: met, set, fan, fun, fat, lip, log, let, had, hit, hen, ship, shop, fish, sack, gof, shup, hib, fot, gock	After 'w' has been taught read and spell: red, run, rat, jog, jet, jam, vet, yap, yes, yum, web, win, wish, wet, sock, yosh, vib, hesh, shib, rof
th z ch q x ng nk	Each day, after each new letter is taught children read and spell: red, run, rat, jog, jet, jam, vet, yap, yes, yum, web, win, wish, wet, sock, yosh, vib, hesh, shib, rof	After 'nk' has been taught read and spell: thin, thick, this, zap, chin, chop, chat, quiz, quit, fox, box, fix, six, sing, bang, thing, wing, chonk, vink, bing, quof, shep
Final set of items for reading and spelling for Speed Sounds Set 1:		
	bell, well, mess, thing, think, wink, blob, blip, brat, drop, drip, clip, from, frog, flag, flop, grin, gran, pram, prop, slip, slid, skip, trip, best, test, bend, jump, send, dress, brop, snom, slonk, frid, crell, stap, scrip, strack, fronp, kitten, kitchen, comic, seven, given, robin, lemon, ribbon, button, jacket, pocket, packet, ticket, rocket, puppet, bucket, carrot, rabbit, cannot	

and two-syllable words, but not vowel digraphs. This final set includes nonwords so that progress can be assessed. The emphasis is on reading, with some spelling. At this point the children who can blend are then given Ditties (Misken, Munton and Archbold, 2011) to read, which have 10 to 20 words of connected text, and contain 'green' (phonic) words and 'red' (common exception/tricky) words.

The children then learn Speed Sounds Set 2: ay, ee, igh, ow, oo (short and long), ar, or, air, ir, ou and oy. This time they are shown words using the new speed sound in the same lesson in which it is taught. For example, when the children learn 'ay', they see words such as 'play' and 'day' on green cards. The children sound and blend each word for reading; for spelling they say the phonemes for the word, pressing their fingers in sequence, and writing the word, e.g. 'play'. They also revise previously taught Speed 1 and 2 letter sounds in each lesson. The reading of appropriate level Storybooks (*Read Write Inc* publication series) starts when the teaching of Set 2 Speed Sounds begins. The Storybooks are read after the children have practised reading the words in them; they read each book three times, firstly to decode the words, secondly so that the teacher can check they have understood the book, and thirdly to discuss the story in greater depth in preparation for planning the writing they will do they next day. Linked to that, work with *Get Writing!* books (Misken, Ruby and Archbold, 2011) is also started, to develop children's writing skills.

The Set 3 items focus on sounds for which there are alternative spellings: 'ea, oi, a-e, i-e, o-e, u-e, aw, are, er, ou ow, ai, oa, ew, ire, ear, ure, tion, cious and tious'. In a lesson the children, for example, revise 'ee' from Speed Sounds Set 2 and learn that 'ea' has the same sound. To do this, they revise words with the 'ee' spelling of the sound, and then read and spell a set of 'ea' words, such as 'clean', and read the appropriate Storybooks.

Altogether, the Speed Sounds cover Phases 2 to 5 inclusive. Speed Sounds 1 covers a lot of Phases 2 to 4 work; Speed Sounds 2 also covers some of Phases 3 and 4, and Speed Sounds 3 covers much of Phase 5, as outlined in *Letters and Sounds*.

When children are reading at the equivalent of National Curriculum Level 2a or above, they are taught using *Read Write Inc Spelling* (Pursglove and Roberts, 2014). This covers Phase 5 vowel digraphs, soft 'c', soft 'g', homophones, suffixes and prefixes. There are also charts for alternative spellings of the same sounds.

Teaching of common exception (tricky) words

In this scheme common exception words are printed on red cards, and so are called 'red' words. These are not used for sight word teaching. The method described on page 47 of the *Phonics Handbook* (Miskin, 2011) for teaching the word 'the' is as follows: 'Hide the red card showing "the"; segment the spoken word into phonemes ("the" -> "th-u"); show children the red card and ask them to look for the tricky letter; show the children "th" is good but "e" is a tricky letter'. These 'red' words are introduced when children start to read connected text in the Ditties. Before reading each Ditty, the children work on the letter sounds, the phonic words (called 'green' words), and any common exception/ tricky ('red') words used in the Ditty.

Pace

The suggested pace for teaching Speed Sounds Set 1 indicates the kind of speed with which phonics can be taught, starting in Reception. On page 36 of the *Phonics Handbook*

(Miskin, 2011), a 'steady' pace of teaching is outlined. In week 1, the letter sounds 'm, a, s, d, t' are taught. From the start of week 2, the children read and spell the words made up from these letters. During weeks 2 to 6 the children learn the rest of the letter sounds from Speed Sounds Set 1, blending and spelling words made up from the letters, as described above. Thus in six weeks this steady pace of teaching covers *Letters and Sounds* Phase 2, and also some of the items in Phase 3, such as the remaining letters of the alphabet and some consonant digraphs (see Table 9.2); it also covers Phase 4, as adjacent consonants are used. A faster pace would see children reaching this point after three weeks of teaching.

Assessment and grouping

This scheme recommends the grouping of children for phonics according to their ability. On page 27 of the *Phonics Handbook* (Miskin, 2011) it is advised that in term 1 of Reception, Set 1 Speed Sounds and Word Time words/nonwords are taught to the whole class for around six weeks, at which point the children can be assessed and grouped according to ability. This is done by using the Sound and Word Entry Assessment (p28), which is grouped into 10 categories. Category A has the letters of the alphabet, in non-alphabetical order; B has CVC words and nonwords; C has consonant digraphs; D has consonant blends; and from E onwards vowel digraphs are tested. Children are tested on several versions of this assessment to see which teaching group is appropriate for them; for each assessment they start at the beginning and read the items until the point where they cannot read any further. The highest level at which they read successfully indicates the sounds that they need to review before progressing. For example, a child may be at level A, knowing few letter sounds, and would need to be taught the Set 1 sounds and Word Time! 1, 2 and 3 again (together with other children performing at the same level). However, a child who is successful on Category C consonant digraphs, being able to sound out most of the words and nonwords, would, with other children performing at around the same level, spend some time reviewing the Set 1 sounds, reviewing the Word Time! lists up to set 5, and then being taught the items in Word Time! 7. In order to deal with ability grouping within the classroom at this early stage, it is recommended that the teacher takes the largest group for 15 to 20 minutes a day, with the teaching assistant taking the smaller group for 15 to 20 minutes, or the teacher takes the two groups in succession. It is also recommended that there is extra small group work for six or seven minutes working on the Set 1 Speed Sounds where needed, using magnetic letters for blending, and rereading the Ditties or Storybooks.

In term 2 of Reception the children are again grouped according to their reading progress, being assessed using Sound and Word Assessment 2 (pp32–3 of the *Phonics Handbook*), which cover the same ground as Assessment 1 but with different items. Once they have been grouped, they spend 30 minutes a day on phonics, with 15 minutes being spent on the Speed Sound lessons, and 15 minutes on text level work. This approach is used also in Term 3, but children work for 30 to 40 minutes a day on phonics and reading text. Groupings can be made across the whole school on ability level using these assessments; for example faster learning Reception children can be grouped with Year 1 children.

Slower learners

Teaching is mixed ability for Speed Sounds Set 1, with the first assessment being carried out at the end of this teaching (after about six weeks using a steady pace). At this point a slower learner group is formed, and the children are thereafter taught according to their ability group.

A SUMMARY OF **KEY POINTS**

➤ *Letters and Sounds* provides a benchmark against which commercial phonics schemes can be assessed.

➤ *Letters and Sounds* provides comprehensive lists of words for teaching phonics in each Phase; the words for Phases 2 to 5 can be found in Appendix 9.

➤ Two commercial programmes are reviewed, *Phonics Bug* and *Read Write Inc*; these cover the phonics needed to prepare children for the Phonics Check.

REFERENCES REFERENCES **REFERENCES** REFERENCES REFERENCES REFERENCES

Betts, H. (2012) *Phonics Bug: Prepare and Assess Handbook*. Harlow: Pearson.

DfE (2013) *The National Curriculum in England*. London: DfE. https://www.gov.uk/government/publications/national-curriculum-in-england-primary-curriculum (retrieved 20 May 2014).

DfES (2007) *Letters and Sounds*. London: DfES. https://www.gov.uk/government/publications/letters-and-sounds (retrieved 27 August 2014).

Johnston, R.S. and Watson, J. (2012) *My Fast Phonics Folder*. Harlow: Pearson.

Miskin, R. (2011) *Read Write Inc Phonics Handbook*. Oxford: Oxford University Press.

Miskin, R., Munton, G. and Archbold, T. (2011) *Read Write Inc Ditty Books*. Oxford: Oxford University Press.

Miskin, R., Ruby, C. and Archbold, T. (2011) *Read Write Inc. Phonics: Get Writing! Handbook*. Oxford: Oxford University Press.

Pursglove, J. and Roberts, J. (2014) *Read Write Inc. Spelling: Teaching Handbook*. Oxford: Oxford University Press.

Standards and Testing Agency (2012) *Phonics Screening Check*. London: DfE. http://media.education.gov.uk/assets/files/pdf/p/phonics%20screening%20check%20sample%20materials.pdf (retrieved 27 August 2014).

TDA (2011) Systematic synthetic phonics in initial teaching training: Guidance and support materials. Notes issued to initial teacher training providers. London: Teaching and Development Agency.

Walker, M., Bartlett, S., Betts, H., Sainsbury, M. and Meta, P. (2013) *Evaluation of the phonics screening check*. NFER research report, May. London: DfE. https://www.gov.uk/government/uploads/system/uploads/attachment_data/file/198994/DFE-RR286A.pdf (retrieved 17 March 2014).

Watson, J.E. and Johnston, R.S. (2010) *Phonics Bug*. Harlow: Pearson.

Adjacent consonants: another term for this is consonant blends; it refers to a sequence of consonants at the beginning or end of words, e.g. <u>cl</u>ap, <u>str</u>ing, po<u>st</u>.

Alphabetic code: this refers to the fact that in English spelling the sounds of the spoken words are represented by letters.

Analytic phonics: this starts by teaching letter sounds at a slow rate (e.g. one a week), in the initial position of words. For example, to teach the letter 'c', children would be shown a series of alliterative words, e.g. '<u>c</u>at', '<u>c</u>ar'. They would then introduced to the letters at the ends of word, e.g. 'nap', 'cup', and then in the middle, e.g. 'c<u>a</u>t', 'b<u>i</u>g'. At this stage, they might be taught to sound and blend. Subsequently initial constant blends, e.g. 'bl', 'cr', final consonant blends, e.g. 'rt', 'lp', then vowel and consonant digraphs, e.g. 'ee', 'ch', would be taught.

Common exception words: see irregular words

Consolidated alphabetic reading: a child recognises larger elements such as morphemes, seeing for example that 'danced' is composed of two morphemes 'dance' and 'ed'.

Consonants: all the letters of the alphabet except the vowels a, e, i, o, u.

Consonant blends: another term for this is adjacent consonants; it refers to a sequence of consonants at the beginning or end of words, e.g. <u>cl</u>ap, <u>str</u>ing, po<u>st</u>.

Consonant digraphs: this is where two consonants are needed to spell one sound, '<u>sh</u>op', '<u>ch</u>ip', '<u>th</u>em'.

Decoding: you can decode many English words by using the sounds of the letters to work out the pronunciation. Many words are *fully decodable*, e.g. 'hat', and some are *partially decodable* (i.e. the spelling is irregular), e.g. 'said'.

Decodable books: these consist of words using the letter sounds that the children have been taught so far. This means that the children can decode (or sound and blend) words in the book with which they are not familiar. There may also be some common exception (tricky) words, which the teacher will teach how to pronounce before the children start each book. New books are introduced as more graphemes are taught. Decodable books for Phase 3 will have a less restricted set of words than decodable books for Phase 2, as more graphemes will have been learnt.

Full alphabetic phase of reading: a child makes connections between letters and sounds all through the word, e.g. the child reads the unfamiliar word 'pat' correctly.

Grapheme: a grapheme is the written representation of a phoneme. Single letters are graphemes, e.g. 't', 'h', but these letters together are also a grapheme, 'th'. For example, the word 'thick' has five letters but only three phonemes 'th' 'i' 'ck'. The term grapheme–phoneme correspondences (GPC) covers letter–sound correspondences, but the latter term refers to the situation where only one letter is needed to represent the sound.

High frequency words: words which occur frequently in written English (i.e. are commonly used). Some of these are regular and some are irregular. According to the National Curriculum, these words are never taught by a 'sight' word approach.

Irregular words: these words have spellings that give a less than perfect guide to pronunciation; they are also called common exception or tricky words. There are two types:

a) Exception words have common spelling patterns (e.g. 'pint', 'have') but their pronunciations differ to most of the words that have similar spellings. For example, 'pint' does not rhyme with 'tint', 'hint', 'splint'; 'have' does not rhyme with 'gave', 'slave', 'wave'.

b) Strange words have unique spellings (e.g. 'yacht', 'gauge', 'aisle') and so are not fully decodable, but have some letter-sound information that corresponds with their pronunciation.

According to the National Curriculum, none of these words should be taught as 'sight' words.

Letter–sound correspondences: the association between the visual representations of letters and their sounds (not their names). Also covered by the term grapheme to phoneme correspondences.

Logographic writing system: a writing system like Chinese, in which individual characters stand for words, but do not represent them pictorially.

Multi-sensory: using sight, touch and sound for learning, particularly of letters.

Morphemes: these are the smallest units of meaning in language and consist of one or more phonemes. All morphemes have meaning, but that meaning can be grammatical. For example, the word 'dog' is a morpheme. We can add the grammatical morpheme 's' to indicate more than one dog, i.e. 'dogs'. A suffix is a morpheme which is added after a word, e.g. 'ing' in 'play<u>ing</u>', which means that play is happening now in the present. In the word 'play<u>ed</u>', the 'ed' means that play happened in the past. A prefix is a morpheme where letters are put before a word to change its meaning, e.g. 'dis' in '<u>dis</u>like' means not, that is, you do not like something.

Nonwords: these are invented words which follow the rules of English spelling but which do not happen to exist. Examples are 'hib', 'flont', 'brin'.

Onset: the onset is the first part of the word, the consonant(s) before the vowel, e.g. in 'bring' the onset is 'br'.

Partial alphabetic phase of reading: a child uses some letter-sound information when reading, often the beginning and/or end letters of words, e.g. a child identifies 'tin' as 'toy'.

Phoneme: this is the smallest sound unit in a word which makes a difference to the word's meaning. For example, you can change the meaning of 'rat' by changing the first phoneme: 'cat', 'mat', 'hat', 'sat'. Therefore /c/, /m/, /h/, /s/ are all phonemes. The term 'phoneme' only refers to sounds, not to written representations (which are graphemes).

Phonics: a method of teaching reading that capitalises on the fact that English spelling is alphabetic. Letter sound or grapheme to phoneme conversion information is used to help pronounce unfamiliar words. The meaning of the term has been extended to include segmenting for spelling.

Phonics Screening Check: a check introduced by the government in England from 2012 to assess whether children at the end of Year 1 (the second year at school) are able to read words and nonwords at the expected level.

Pre-alphabetic phase of reading: a child reads words by salient visual cues and does not look at the letters. It is sometimes referred to as logographic reading. For example, a child may recognise 'Pepsi' correctly when the word is presented with its logo and distinctive lettering. However, if the letter 'p' is replaced by the letter 'x', so it is shown as 'Xepsi', the child still reads it as 'Pepsi'.

Phonemic awareness: the ability to perceive and manipulate the phonemes in *spoken* words. If you were testing a child's explicit phoneme awareness, you would read out words to them, and they would tell you the phonemes in the word. That is, they would tell you that the spoken word 'cat' has the sounds /c/ /a/ /t/. They would not be looking at the printed words while they were doing this task.

Phonological awareness: the ability to perceive and manipulate the sounds of spoken words. It includes the smallest level, phonemes, but also larger units, such as rimes and syllables.

Pseudowords: see nonwords

Regular words: the pronunciations of these words are predictable on the basis of simple grapheme to phoneme conversion rules, for example, 'cat', 'best', 'hand'. These words are completely decodable through sounding and blending.

Rime: the rime of a word is the vowel and the rest of the syllable, e.g. in 'bring' the rime is 'ing'.

Segmenting for spelling: splitting a spoken word into phonemes, and selecting the letter(s) for each phoneme in order to spell the word. According to the National Curriculum, even after Key Stage 1 'teachers should still draw pupils' attention to GPCs that do and do not fit in with what has been taught so far'. This means that the spelling of high frequency and common exception (tricky) words should not be taught by a sight approach.

Sight-word reading: there are many uses of this term. It can refer to a global recognition of words where little use is made of letter-sound information (sometimes called logographic reading). However, Ehri describes how sight-word reading becomes more mature during reading development by being increasingly underpinned by letter-sound information. However, she proposes that even when a word becomes very familiar, and can be recognised without overtly using the letter sounds, we still activate not only its whole word pronunciation, but all the possible connections between letters and sounds (for example, the connections between the letters and onsets and rimes, and also the connections between the letters and each individual phoneme).

Simple view of reading: reading comprehension can be predicted by multiplying together the ability to a) recognise and decode printed words, and b) to understand spoken language.

Sounding and blending for reading: when trying to read an unfamiliar word the child generates the sounds of the letters (or graphemes) from left to right, and then blends them together to find out how the word is pronounced.

Syllables: a syllable is a word or part of a word that can be spoken independently. For example, 'alphabet' has three syllables, al/pha/bet. Syllables can be spelt by one letter or a group of letters (e.g. 'a', 'I', 'cat', 'boat', 'my'). All words have at least one syllable and each syllable has one vowel sound (vowel digraphs count as one vowel, and 'y' can count as a vowel).

Synthetic phonics: starts by teaching children a small group of letter sounds very rapidly, e.g. s, a, t, i, p, n. Children sound and blend words made up of the taught letters to find out how to pronounce them. Then another letter sound is taught, and children sound and blend new words made up of the previously taught letters. This process continues until all of the letter sounds, digraphs etc. used in English, have been taught.

Tricky words: these are common exception (irregular) words, where the letter sounds do not provide a perfect guide to pronunciation, e.g. 'said'. Some words are temporarily classified as 'tricky' even though they have regular spellings; this is because the word is used in decodable readers before the relevant phonics teaching has taken place. For example, the word 'like' will be introduced before children have learnt about split digraphs. According to the National Curriculum children are never taught to recognise any of these words by 'sight', their attention is drawn to the decodable and partially decodable elements.

Vowels: there can be as many as 20 vowels in spoken English (the number depends on accent). These are represented in spelling by the letters of the alphabet a, e, i, o, u, either singly or in pairs (see vowel digraphs below). Sometimes 'y' can be used as a vowel, e.g. in 'my'.

Vowel digraphs: some vowel sounds are spelt using two vowels, e.g. 'oa' in 'coat'. A special set of vowel digraphs are variously called silent 'e', magic 'e', or split digraphs. These terms all refer to where the sound of a vowel is lengthened by adding an 'e' after the final consonant, e.g. 'late', 'cube'.

Whole language: the whole language approach grew from work by Ken Goodman in the 1960s; his work led to the idea that children did not need to learn to decode unfamiliar words using the letter sounds, but that they could be guessed from context. Frank Smith thought that children should be immersed in 'real books', the view being that 'children learn to read by reading'.

Appendix 1: Graphophonemic Awareness Training for Adults

1 Test yourself

Try identifying the letter(s) which represent the phonemes in these words. Here are some examples:

D<u>O</u>G 3   S<u>H</u>I<u>P</u> 3   S<u>KAT</u>E 4   <u>M</u>E<u>AT</u> 3   <u>R</u>U<u>MP</u> 4   <u>B</u>O<u>M</u>B 3

Say the following words to yourself. Look at the letters in each word and circle or underline which letter(s) correspond to each phoneme. In the blank following the word, record the number of phonemes you detected.

Your attempt			Your attempt		
TYPE A			Type E		
clam	CLAM	_____	chop	CHOP	_____
slit	SLIT	_____	cash	CASH	_____
skip	SKIP	_____	thin	THIN	_____
flog	FLOG	_____	moth	MOTH	_____
plod	PLOD	_____	chin	CHIN	_____
TYPE B			**TYPE F**		
salt	SALT	_____	came	CAME	_____
list	LIST	_____	swede	SWEDE	_____
bank	BANK	_____	hide	HIDE	_____
hulk	HULK	_____	rose	ROSE	_____
lump	LUMP	_____	cute	CUTE	_____
TYPE C			**TYPE G**		
fit	FIT	_____	knife	KNIFE	_____
hug	HUG	_____	gnat	GNAT	_____
sap	SAP	_____	gnome	GNOME	_____
led	LED	_____	wreck	WRECK	_____
hop	HOP	_____	knew	KNEW	_____
TYPE D			**TYPE H**		
goat	GOAT	_____	phonics	PHONICS	_____
sail	SAIL	_____	orphan	ORPHAN	_____
lies	LIES	_____	prophet	PROPHET	_____
crow	CROW	_____	morph	MORPH	_____
bean	BEAN	_____	pheasant	PHEASANT	_____

2 Check your answers

TYPE A

clam	C L A M	4
slit	S L I T	4
skip	S K I P	4
flog	F L O G	4
plod	P L O D	4

TYPE B

salt	S A L T	4
list	L I S T	4
bank	B A N K	4
hulk	H U L K	4
lump	L U M P	4

TYPE C

fit	F I T	3
hug	H U G	3
sap	S A P	3
led	L E D	3
hop	H O P	3

TYPE D

goat	G O A T	3
sail	S A I L	3
lies	L I E S	3
crow	C R O W	3
bean	B E A N	3

Type E

chop	C H O P	3
cash	C A S H	3
thin	T H I N	3
moth	M O T H	3
chin	C H I N	3

TYPE F

came	C A M E	3
swede	S W E D E	4
hide	H I D E	3
rose	R O S E	3
cute	C U T E	3

TYPE G

knife	K N I F E	3
gnat	G N A T	3
gnome	G N O M E	3
wreck	W R E C K	3
knew	K N E W	2

TYPE H

phonics	P H O N I C S	6
orphan	O R P H A N	4
(Scottish	*O R P H A N*	*5)*
prophet	P R O P H E T	6
morph	M O R P H	3
(Scottish	*M O R P H*	*4)*
pheasant	P H E A S A N T	6

Errors typically made on these word types

A. Initial consonant blends treated as one sound, e.g. cl am; vowel and following consonant treated as one sound, e.g. cl am.

B. Final consonant blends treated as one sound, e.g. sa lt; consonant and following vowel treated as one sound, e.g. sa lt.

C. Initial consonants put together with the following vowel, e.g. fi t; vowel and following consonant treated as one sound, e.g. f it.

D. Vowel digraphs treated as two sounds, e.g. g o a t; first letter of vowel digraph underlined as the letter name gives the vowel sound, e.g. g o a t

E. Consonant digraphs treated as two sounds, e.g. c h op.

F. Silent e's underlined (the 'e' in split digraphs), e.g. came.

G. Silent letters underlined, e.g. g n a t.

H. The letters in the consonant digraph 'ph' underlined separately, e.g. p h on i c s.

Appendix 2: Phoneme Awareness Training Programme for Children

We do not ourselves advocate teaching phoneme awareness without letters, but the following lessons will aid the implementation of Phase 1, aspect 7 (oral blending and segmenting), where this is felt to be appropriate. These lessons are based on the training programme we used in Johnston and Watson (2004, Experiment 1).

Throughout this training programme children are not shown the letters that represent the sounds that are being learnt. We recommend the use of a hand puppet to demonstrate the procedures.

Lesson 1 Segmenting the initial phoneme in spoken words

Note: ' ' denotes the whole spoken word; / / denotes the sounds

1. Explain to the children that they are going to play with the first sound in words; the puppet and children will need to listen very carefully for the first sound of each word.
2. Present a three-box phoneme frame, as below, which can be drawn in chalk on the blackboard. Make a puppet slide a finger under the three squares of the frame saying 'mop' in an elongated way. Ask the puppet for the first sound; the puppet says 'The first sound in "mop" is /m/' and points to the first box. Ask the puppet to put in a large dot.

3. Repeat the process for the word 'hop' asking one of the pupils to assist the puppet.
4. Repeat the process for the word 'cat' asking one of the children to perform without the help of the puppet (unless required).
5. Repeat the process with all of the children marking their sheets with a large dot for the first sound of the words in the list as you go through each word. Give support in saying the first sound if necessary.

Word list

The letters between slash marks indicate it is the sound as it occurs at the start of the word that is to be used, not the letter name.

top – /t/	dad – /d/
pot – /p/	cut – /c/
nip – /n/	get – /g/
it – /i/	leg – /l/
sat – /s/	fun – /f/
rip – /r/	old – /o/
mug – /m/	bit – /b/

6. At the end of the lesson remind the children of what has been learnt, i.e. to say the first sound heard at the beginning of a word.

Lesson 2 Segmenting the final phoneme in spoken words

First of all revise initial sound segmentation from the previous lesson.

Now the children will learn to say the last sound of a word, represented by the last square of the frame.

1. Explain that they are going to play with the last sound in words; the puppet and children will need to listen very carefully for the last sound of each word.
2. The puppet slides a finger under the three boxes of the frame saying 'mop'. Ask the puppet what is the last sound; the puppet says /p/. Ask the puppet to point to the last box, say the last sound again, and put in a large dot.
3. Repeat the process for the word 'pot', asking one of the pupils to assist the puppet.
4. Repeat the process for 'cat' asking one of the pupils to perform without the help of the puppet (unless required).
5. Repeat the process for each of the remainder of the given words for that day asking other children to perform without the help of the puppet (unless required). They should put a dot in the last box as they segment the sound.

top – /p/	dad – /d/	gas – /s/	fill – /l/
bit – /t/	luck – /k/	fur – /r/ (optional)	cough – /f/
fin – /n/	fig – /g/	ham – /m/	cub – /b/

6. Remind the children of what has been learnt, i.e. to hear the sound at the end of words.

Lesson 3 Segmenting first and final phonemes in spoken words

Remind the children that in the previous lesson they found the last sounds in words. This lesson includes nonwords. Nonwords are made-up words; you can tell the children that they are made up and do not make sense.

1. Use the three-box frame as before. The puppet slides a finger under the three squares of the frame saying 'mop'. Ask the puppet what is the first sound of 'mop'; the puppet says /m/, points to the first box and puts in a large dot.
2. Ask the puppet what is the last sound of the word 'mop' and the puppet will say the last sound is /p/, point to the last box and put in a large dot.
3. Repeat the process for the word 'pot', asking one of the children to assist the puppet, saying /p/ is the first sound and /t/ is the last sound.
4. Repeat the process for the word 'cat' asking one of the pupils to perform without the help of the puppet (unless required), '/c/ is the first sound and /t/ is the last sound.'
5. Repeat the process for the following words, asking the children to say the sounds without the help of the puppet (unless required), marking the boxes with large dots.
   Further words and nonwords to work through:

   mac, name, cot, log, book, bim, bat, cos, gob, sip, pub, top, nog, foot, pon, mot, bag, mag, pass, nap, map, tab, pac, sab, cas, toc, gop

6. Remind the pupils of what has been learnt, i.e. to say the first and the last sound in words.

Lesson 4 Deleting initial and final phonemes and saying what sound is left

The children will learn to segment the final sound and say what is left of the word, and then segment the initial sound and say what is left of the word.

a) Phoneme segmentation

Say 'Now we are going to find the first and last sounds in the word "cot".' (Run the puppet's finger under the boxes as you say 'cot').

'What is the last sound of "cot"? It's /t/.' Put a dot in the last box.

'What is the first sound of "cot" ? It's /c/.' Put a dot in the first box.

b) Phoneme deletion

Then say 'What sound is left if you take the "c" from "cot"? It's /ot/.' Run your finger under the last two boxes as you say /ot/.

'What sound is there if you take the /t/ from "cot"? It's /co/.' Run your finger under the first two boxes as you say /co/.

Repeat a) and b) using the following examples, firstly finding the first and last sounds (phoneme segmentation), and then saying what is left in each word after these sounds are in turn taken off (phoneme deletion).

The segments to pronounce for b) are given below:

cat – 'cat' without the /t/ is /ca/, 'cat' without the /c/ is /at/

dip – 'dip' without the /p/ is /di/, 'dip' without the /d/ is /ip/

sun – 'sun' without the /n/ is /su/, 'sun' without the /s/ is /un/

fuss – 'fuss' without the /s/ is /fu/, 'fuss' without the /f/ is /uss/

purr – (optional) 'purr' without the /r/ is /pu/, 'purr' without the /p/ is /ur/

gum – 'gum' without the /m/ is 'gu', 'gum' without the /g/ is /um/

rod – 'rod' without the /d/ is /ro/, 'rod' without the /r/ is /od/

tick – 'tick' without the /k/ is /ti/, 'tick' without the /t/ is /ik/

leg – 'leg' without the /g/ is /le/, 'leg' without the /l/ is /eg/

fell – 'fell' without the /l/ is /fe/, 'fell' without the /f/ is /el/

buff – 'buff' without the /f/ is /bu/, 'buff' without the /b/ is /uff/

sob – 'sob' without the /b/ is /so/, 'sob' without the /s/ is /ob/

mat – 'mat' without the /t/ is /ma/, 'mat' without the /m/ is /at/

nap – 'nap' without the /p/ is /na/, 'nap' without the /n/ is /ap/

Remind the children of what they have learnt today: to take sounds off words and to say what is left.

Lesson 5 Segmenting vowels at the beginning of words

This lesson uses vowel-consonant nonwords (VC). Nonwords are made-up words; you can tell the children that they are made up and do not make sense.

Remind children that in Lesson 4 they learnt to take the first sound off a word and say what was left, and then to take off the final sound and say what was left.

1. Ask the children to listen carefully. You say the word 'at', the puppet slides a finger under the two boxes of the frame saying 'at'. Ask the children to listen for the first sound in 'at'. The puppet points to the first box and says 'The first sound is /a/, /a/ is a vowel.' The puppet puts a large dot in the first box.
2. Repeat the process saying the nonword 'ag' with a child helping the puppet.
3. Repeat the process with the puppet saying the word 'of' and a child pointing to the first box, saying the first vowel sound /o/ independently. (Give help if necessary.)
4. Repeat this process for the series of words listed. In every case the /a/ vowel sound is as in 'apple', the /o/ vowel sound is as in 'odd', the /i/ sound as in 'it', the /u/ sound as in 'cup', the /e/ sound as in 'get'. The children will mark the position of the vowel with a large dot on their phoneme frames.
   List of vowel-consonant nonwords to use

   ot, am, im, eb, ug, ob, ip, ek, ub, em, ak, op, at, ib, ut, es, ik, og, ev, ul, ep, ab, om, ok, as, id, um, ig, un

5. Remind the children of what they have been learning, finding the first vowel sound in short words.

Lesson 6 Segmenting vowels from the end of words

Remind the children that in the previous lesson they learnt to identify vowels at the beginning of nonwords.

1. Tell the children they are now going to listen for vowels at the end of words. Ask the children to listen carefully. The puppet slides a finger under the frame and says 'sa' (pronounced as in 'sat'). Ask the children to listen for the last sound in 'sa'. The puppet points to the last box and says 'The last sound is /a/', and put in a large dot.
2. Repeat the process saying the nonword 'po' (as in 'pod'), with a child helping the puppet.
3. Repeat the process with the puppet saying the nonword 'ma' (as in 'mat'), and a child pointing to the last box, saying independently 'The last sound is /a/.' (Give help if necessary).
4. Repeat this process for the series of words listed, the children putting a large dot in the last box on their sheets as each vowel is segmented. The vowel sounds are pronounced as in Lesson 5.
   List of CV nonwords

   pa, ke, nu, ga, bo, te, pu, mi, de, ko, ta, tu, di, le, ba, du, so, si, ga, ne, ru, pa, pi, bu, fe, bo, ki, mo

5. Remind the children of what they have been learning, i.e. segmenting the vowel sound in nonwords.

Lesson 7 Segmenting phonemes in the middle of words

Remind the children that we have been listening for vowel sounds as first and last sounds. Today, we are listening for the vowel sounds in the middle of words.

1. Using the three-box frame, say the word 'bat', the puppet sliding a finger along underneath while saying the word 'bat'. Ask the children to listen carefully for the middle sound. Say the word 'bat', and ask 'What is the middle sound?' The puppet points to the middle box in the frame and says 'The middle sound is /a/', and puts a large dot in the middle box.

   If this is difficult, tell the children to take off the first sound and see what is left. 'Let's see what "bat" without the /b/ is – it's "at". Now what is "at" without the /t/ – it's /a/.'

2. Repeat the process saying the word 'fob' with a child helping the puppet. 'What is the middle sound in "fob"? It's /o/.'
3. Repeat the process with the puppet saying the word 'bam'. Ask what is the middle sound in 'bam'. A child independently points to the middle box saying the middle sound is /a/. (Give help where necessary.)
4. Repeat the process for the series of words listed, the children putting a large dot in the middle box of their three-box frames as each vowel is identified.
   List of words

   back, knob, cab, sob, cat, gop, tack, mag, cot, mab, cop, tob, bag, pob, lock, mass, tack, pal, poc, top, pan, hab, mot, tag, cut, mof, pass, sock, tap, pot, net, sun, ant, dog, hat, cup, man, rat

5. Remind the children of what they have been learning, i.e. listening to words and saying the middle sound in each word.

Lesson 8 Segmenting all the phonemes in CVC (consonant-vowel-consonant) words

In this lesson the children will learn to segment the initial, middle and final sounds of words. Remind the children that last time they were finding the middle sounds of words.

1. Using the three-box frame, say the word 'pot', sliding the puppet's finger under the frame. Point to each of the boxes in turn, saying the sounds /p/ /o/ /t/.
2. Repeat the process and when you point to each of the boxes in turn, the puppet says the first sound is /p/, the middle sound is /o/, and the last sound is /t/. Put a large dot in each box as the phoneme is pronounced.
3. Repeat the process for the non-word 'tas'. The puppet and a child say the first sound is /t/, the middle sound is /a/ and the last sound is /s/.
4. Repeat the process for the word 'cab'. A child says 'The first sound is /c/ the middle sound is /a/ and the last sound is /b/.' (Give help where necessary).
5. Repeat the process with the children filling in the dots on their three-box frames for the words in the list:

   top, cot, bab, mac, sam, bat, got, cat, mac, tom, bot, pot, tam, sap, mat, pat, mag, sog, pom, gop, sot, cag, pos, cog, pob, pub, cab, dig, hen, fat, ant, pan, dog, hat, lum, cos, sog, sop

6. Remind the children that they have been listening to words and saying what is the first sound, the middle sound and the last sound.

Lesson 9 Auditory blending: blending the last phoneme of a word with the rest of the word, as in 'ca-t'.

Remind the children that last time they were learning about finding the first, middle and end sounds in words, using the word 'cat' as an example. Now the children are going to blend all the sounds together to make a word.

1. Tell the children they will hear words broken into small parts; they are going to blend these parts together to make a whole word. Ask the children to listen while the puppet slides its finger under the first two boxes, saying /ba/, then under box 3, saying /g/.
2. Then slide the puppet's finger under all three boxes, saying 'bag' in an elongated way but without any breaks. Then say the whole word normally, 'bag', and then put it in a sentence, e.g. 'Put the towel in the bag'.
3. Repeat the process for /ta/ /s/ with the puppet saying the sounds /ta/ /s/ separately, then the whole non-word 'tas', then saying 'Tas is a nonsense word'.
4. Repeat the process with the puppet and a child for the segments /mo/ /p/, saying the sounds separately, then the word 'mop' in an elongated way, and then normally 'mop', and then a sentence – 'We use a mop to clean the floor.'
5. Repeat the process for the words in the list:

   ma-ss, go-p, ba-ck, sa-ck, ca-p, ta-g, so-b, to-m, ba-g, ca-t, po-c, ba-m, ga-b, po-t, ta-ck, so-ck, so-p, ma-p, sa-p, ca-b, ca-t, pa-ck, ga-s, so-b, mo-p, ta-ck, ba-g, pa-ss, so-ck

6. Remind the children that we have been blending the last sound of the word with the rest of the word.

Lesson 10 Blending initial phonemes with the rest of the word

Remind the children that last time they blended the last sound of a word with the rest of the word. Say 'Today, we are going to blend the first sound of a word with the rest of the word.'

1. Ask the children to listen while the puppet slides its finger under one box, saying /c/, and then under the last two boxes, saying /ap/.
2. Slide the puppet's finger under all three boxes saying 'cap', followed by a sentence, e.g. 'I took off my cap.'
3. Repeat the process with the puppet saying the sounds /g/ /om/ and then the nonword 'gom', followed by the sentence 'Gom is a nonsense word.'
4. Repeat the process with the puppet and a child saying the sounds /g/ /as/ and then 'gas', finally using the word 'gas' in a sentence, e.g. 'We cook using gas.'
5. Repeat the process for the words in the list with children saying the sounds and the word, and you giving a sentence. Do not say the whole word first!

   m-at, g-ot, s-ack, c-ap, t-ag, s-ob, t-op, b-ag, c-at, p-oc, b-am, g-ab, p-ass, p- ot, t-ack, s-ock, s-op, m-ap

6. Remind the children that we have been blending the first sound of the word with the rest of the word to make the word.

Lesson 11 Bending three separate phonemes into a word, as in 'c-a-t'

Remind the children that we have been blending the last sound of a word with the rest of the word, and the first sound of a word with the rest of the word. Today, we are going to say all three sounds and blend them into a word.

1. Say that the puppet is going to speak in sound-talk, and we are going to work out what it is saying. The puppet says the sounds /m/ /a/ /t/, while pointing to each box in turn. Then the puppet blends the sounds to say 'mat'.
2. The puppet gives the sounds /h/ /a/ /t/, the children copy the sounds, and then the puppet and the children blend the sounds together.
3. Repeat this process for each of the words in the list:

   sun, tap, pin, net, pig, bus, leg, bed, jam, van, mat, ant, hen, fan, cup, fox, tin, cat, dog

4. Remind the children that we have been saying blending sounds together to find out what the word is.

Lesson 12 Segmenting spoken words into phonemes and blending them back together

Remind the children that last time they sound-talked the words and then blended the sounds together. Tell the children 'You are now going to take a word, cut it up into sound-talk, and then put it back together again. Blending the sounds will change them a bit, but you should still be able to hear them.'

1. The puppet says the word 'bag'.
2. Ask the puppet to put it in sound-talk – the puppet says /b/ /a/ /g/.
3. Ask the puppet to put it back together. The puppet says 'bag' in an elongated way, running its finger under the boxes, and then says 'bag' normally.
4. Then the puppet and the children do the same procedure with 'gas' /g/ /a/ /s/. Blend it together in an elongated way, 'gas', while the puppet runs its finger under the boxes. Then say 'gas' normally.
5. Ask the children what are the sounds in 'tap' – see if they can say /t/ /a/ /p/, but help them if they cannot do this. Then ask them to blend the sounds together (assist them if they cannot do this).
6. Repeat this process with the following words:

   tap, pin, get, rat, man, rim, pat, men, pan, cap, kit, nap, tan, dig, gap, peg, pal, tin, sat, sip, pal, kin, rap, pit, man, rip, mat, leg, tip, can, sit, ran, ten, pen, cat

7. Remind them of what they have been doing in the lesson, blending sounds together to see what the word is.

On the following pages are some two- and three-box phoneme frames that you can photocopy to give to the children.

Name _____ Date _____

Name _____ Date _____

Appendix 3: Score sheet to assess children's knowledge of the letters s a t p

Date: Child's name	Alphabet knowledge				Can give the sound for:				Can write letters for:			
	Song		With print		's'	'a'	't'	'p'	/s/	/a/	/t/	/p/
	Yes	No	Yes	No								

Appendix 4: Score sheet to assess children's ability to sound and blend the letters s a t p

| | Blending | | | | | Blending | | | Alphabet | | | | Segmentation | | |
| | | | | | | | | | Song Print | | | | Dictation | | Picture |
Date: Child's name	as	at	sap	sat	tap	taps	pat	pats	Y	N	Y	N	pats	taps	tap

Appendix 5: Rules for where to split words into syllables

	Rule	Example
1	If two consonants are together between two vowels, the first syllable usually ends *after* the first consonant. (For dividing a word into syllables, a consonant blend or a consonant digraph is considered as one consonant. Never split up consonant digraphs as they represent only one sound.)	car / ton yel / low pitch / er 'ch' 'ph' 'sh' 'th' 'th' and 'wh'
2	If a consonant is followed by the ending 'le' the split is *before* the consonant. (Exception: 'ckle' words like pick / le)	pur / ple tum / ble
3	When a word has 'ck' or 'x' in it, the split is usually after the 'ck' or 'x'.	pack / et tax / i
4	A compound word is split between the two words making the compound word.	flash / light down / stairs
5	Vowel digraphs and vowel combinations count as one sound.	count dough / nut
6	If a syllable ends in a vowel (any vowel) and is the only vowel, it is usually long.	o / pen pa / per
7	If a root word has a prefix, split the word *after* the prefix.	re / play un / load
8	If a root word has a suffix, split the word *between* the root word and the suffix. (When the suffix 'ing' is added to a one-syllable word, the last consonant is doubled before adding 'ing'.)	play / ing read / ing
9	'ed' coming at the end of a word only forms a syllable when preceded by 'd' or 't'.	dart / ed print / ed
10	A syllable ending in a silent 'e' has one and only one consonant before that silent 'e'. Silent 'e' does not count as a syllable.	plan and plane are both one syllable

Appendix 6: Hull Diagnostic Phonics Checks 1 and 2

These two tests are designed to be diagnostic and so cover a wider range of phonics than the government Phonics Screening Checks. In particular, they include some vowel digraphs that have variable pronunciations. There are some notes on the score sheets about acceptable variations in the pronunciation of pseudowords; you may spot other possible pronunciations that are correct in English words! These words and nonwords should be shown to children in the Sassoon Infant font, 48 pitch, to be compatible with the presentation of items in the Phonics Screening Check. The idea is to write down the children's responses for later analysis, to target catch-up work.

Instructions for administration to children

1. 'We are going to look at some words and made-up words. Say them out loud as best you can.'
2. Using a sheet of paper, reveal the items one by one.
3. Before testing the words say 'These are real words.'
4. Before testing the pseudowords say 'These are made-up words.'
5. If the child makes an incorrect response and then they correct it mark this as correct. If the child makes several attempts at an item, note down the final attempt to guide what remediation is needed. Note whether they just sounded out the phonemes and did not blend, as this is an indicator that further work is needed on blending. Where the phonemes are sounded out incorrectly, note these down and then give the child extra work on these grapheme–phoneme correspondences.

Practice items for both Hull Diagnostic Phonics Checks

These items should be shown to the children in the Sassoon Infant font, 48 pitch.

Use the same instructions as for the diagnostic test, but do not score the answers.

cat

dog

top

pip

lig

dal

nos

mep

Hull Diagnostic Phonics Check 1

These items should be shown to the children in the Sassoon Infant font, 48 pitch.

Section 1	Section 2
hem	what
bun	pine
flick	tube
cuff	hedge
hiss	pay
seen	rate
soon	graph
lead	haul
shorn	twirl
hair	Chris
jud	fene
fosh	gly
frib	zeer
crull	datch
zunk	mied
yeed	doke
woat	plew
chark	cem
quob	wouth
mern	geb

Hull Diagnostic Phonics Check 1 score sheet

Child's name _____   **Date** _____

Section 1 (Reception)

Words	Child's response	Give tick if correct
hem		
bun		
flick		
cuff		
hiss		
seen		
soon		
lead		
shorn		
hair		

Pseudowords	Child's response	Give tick if correct
jud (as in 'mud')		
fosh (as in 'gosh')		
frib (as in 'crib')		
crull (as in 'dull' or as in 'pull')		
zunk (as in 'dunk')		
yeed (as in 'need')		
woat (as in 'moat')		
chark (could be 'ch' as in 'church', or 'ch' as in 'choir')		
quob (as in 'fob')		
mern (as in 'fern')		

Section 2 (Key Stage 1)

Words	Child's response	Give tick if correct
what		
pine		
tube		
hedge		
pay		
rate		
graph		
haul		
twirl		
Chris		

Pseudowords	Child's response	Give tick if correct
fene (as in 'scene')		
gly (as in 'fly')		
zeer (as in 'beer')		
datch (as in 'match')		
mied (as in 'tied', could be as in 'shield')		
doke (as in 'poke')		
plew (as in 'flew')		
cem (as /s/ in 'sem')		
wouth (as in 'mouth')		
geb (as /j/ in 'jeb')		

Hull Diagnostic Phonics Check 2

These items should be shown to the children in the Sassoon Infant font, 48 pitch.

Section 1	Section 2
hop	Eve
dish	fly
clip	deer
tell	latch
pain	tied
load	poke
sharp	stew
quit	cent
need	mouth
here	gem
pag	wheg
nim	rine
cleck	mube
haff	bedge
dess	vay
poin	dabe
jigh	phid
zoog	taud
shorp	firt
kair	chrob

Hull Diagnostic Phonics Check 2 score sheet

Child's name _____   **Date** _____

Section 1 (Reception)

Words	Child's response	Give tick if correct
hop		
dish		
clip		
tell		
pain		
load		
sharp		
quit		
need		
herb		

Pseudowords	Child's response	Give tick if correct
pag (as in 'nag')		
nim (as in 'him')		
cleck (as in 'fleck')		
haff (as in 'chaff')		
dess (as in 'less')		
poin (as in 'coin')		
jigh (as in 'high')		
zoog (short oo as in 'foot', or long oo as in 'moon')		
shorp		
kair (as in 'hair')		

Section 2 (Key Stage 1)

Words	Child's response	Give tick if correct
Eve		
fly		
deer		
latch		
tied		
poke		
stew		
cent		
mouth		
gem		

Pseudowords	Child's response	Give tick if correct
wheg (as in 'weg', but could be 'h' as in 'who', i.e. 'heg')		
rine (as in 'mine')		
mube (as in 'tube')		
bedge (as in 'hedge')		
vay (as in 'way')		
dabe (as in 'babe')		
phid (as in 'fib')		
taud (as in 'haunt')		
firt (as in 'third')		
chrob (ch as in 'church', or ch as in 'choir')		

Appendix 7: Nonwords for testing and assessing

These items should be shown to the children in the Sassoon Infant font, 48 pitch, to be compatible with the Phonics Screening Check.

a) Nonwords for testing sounding and blending in Phases 2 and 3

Child's name _____   **Date** _____

Child's response

Child's response

hig _____	gantok _____
nal _____	muntal _____
kug _____	renbok _____
bis _____	sanlud _____
gok _____	minlan _____
dep _____	ritney _____
foy _____	yomter _____
kun _____	nusdal _____
ged _____	daspog _____
lar _____	ludpon _____
jek _____	bosdin _____
lan _____	culgin _____
mip _____	fambey _____
pos _____	kesdal _____
ruk _____	libnol _____
dal _____	bantik _____
ped _____	lemfid _____
fik _____	mitson _____
lom _____	goklup _____
sul _____	puklon _____

b) Nonwords for assessing phonics skills for Phases 3 and 4 (adjacent consonants and some vowel digraphs)

Child's name _____

Date _____

Child's response		**Child's response**	
sned	_____	fost	_____
clom	_____	hald	_____
spad	_____	nard	_____
frod	_____	noip	_____
stod	_____	kust	_____
pran	_____	folt	_____
grik	_____	wolp	_____
plud	_____	kants	_____
drot	_____	bork	_____
smid	_____	noot	_____
glat	_____	lind	_____
flup	_____	benk	_____

c) Nonwords for testing Phase 5 (vowel digraphs)

Some vowel digraphs by this stage have multiple acceptable pronunciations, for example, 'kear' could rhyme with 'year' or 'bear'.

Child's name _____   **Date** _____

Child's response		**Child's response**	
poad	_____	dife	_____
kear	_____	noke	_____
yied	_____	cose	_____
doud	_____	wone	_____
yawt	_____	pake	_____
kirt	_____	fube	_____
nowd	_____	sode	_____
noy	_____	pone	_____
baum	_____	lude	_____
cait	_____	nade	_____
vay	_____	bime	_____
surm	_____	neke	_____

Appendix 8: Catch-up sheets to be used with the Hull Diagnostic Phonics Checks (Appendix 6) and the Nonword Reading Tests (Appendix 7)

Circle graphemes on which child is having difficulty; you can then see if the problems are with simple letter–sound correspondences, consonant digraphs, adjacent consonants or vowel digraphs, and so on. You can form a nurture group of children needing the same sort of extra help.

	Phase 2 Reception							Phase 3 Reception	
Letters and Sounds order	Set 1	Set 2	Set 3	Set 4	Set 5	Set 6	Set 7	New graphemes	
Child's name	s a t p	i n m d	g o c k	ck e u r	h b f ff l ll ss	j v w x	y z zz qu	ch sh th ng	ai ee igh oa short/long oo
	s a t p	i n m d	g o c k	ck e u r	h b f ff l ll ss	j v w x	y z zz qu	ch sh th ng	ai ee igh oa short/long oo
	s a t p	i n m d	g o c k	ck e u r	h b f ff l ll ss	j v w x	y z zz qu	ch sh th ng	ai ee igh oa short/long oo
	s a t p	i n m d	g o c k	ck e u r	h b f ff l ll ss	j v w x	y z zz qu	ch sh th ng	ai ee igh oa short/long oo
	s a t p	i n m d	g o c k	ck e u r	h b f ff l ll ss	j v w x	y z zz qu	ch sh th ng	ai ee igh oa short/long oo
	s a t p	i n m d	g o c k	ck e u r	h b f ff l ll ss	j v w x	y z zz qu	ch sh th ng	ai ee igh oa short/long oo
.	s a t p	i n m d	g o c k	ck e u r	h b f ff l ll ss	j v w x	y z zz qu	ch sh th ng	ai ee igh oa short/long oo

Child's name	Phase 3 Reception New graphemes		Phase 4 Reception	Phase 5 Year 1 New graphemes for reading					
Letters and Sounds order	ar or ur ow oi	ear air ure er	Adjacent consonants (CVCC, CCV, CCVC, CCVCC, CCCVCC and CCCVCC words)	zh wh ph	ay a-e eigh ey ei	ea e-e ie ey y	ie i-e y i	ow o-e o/ oe	ew ue u-e u oul
	ar or ur ow oi	ear air ure er		zh wh ph	ay a-e eigh ey ei	ea e-e ie ey y	ie i-e y i	ow o-e o/ oe	ew ue u-e u oul
	ar or ur ow oi	ear air ure er		zh wh ph	ay a-e eigh ey ei	ea e-e ie ey y	ie i-e y i	ow o-e o/ oe	ew ue u-e u oul
	ar or ur ow oi	ear air ure er		zh wh ph	ay a-e eigh ey ei	ea e-e ie ey y	ie i-e y i	ow o-e o/ oe	ew ue u-e u oul
	ar or ur ow oi	ear air ure er		zh wh ph	ay a-e eigh ey ei	ea e-e ie ey y	ie i-e y i	ow o-e o/ oe	ew ue u-e u oul
	ar or ur ow oi	ear air ure er		zh wh ph	ay a-e eigh ey ei	ea e-e ie ey y	ie i-e y i	ow o-e o/ oe	ew ue u-e u oul
	ar or ur ow oi	ear air ure er		zh wh ph	ay a-e eigh ey ei	ea e-e ie ey y	ie i-e y i	ow o-e o/ oe	ew ue u-e u oul

Phase 5 Year 1

Letters and Sounds order									
Child's name	**aw au al**	**ir er ear (as in earth)**	**ou oy**	**ere eer are ear (as in pear)**	**c k ck ch**	**ce ci cy sc stl se**	**ge gi gy dge**	**le mb kn gn wr**	**tch sh (as in action) ea (as in head) (w)a**
	aw au al	ir er ear (as in earth)	ou oy	ere eer are ear (as in pear)	c k ck ch	ce ci cy sc stl se	ge gi gy dge	le mb kn gn wr	tch sh (as in action) ea (as in head) (w)a
	aw au al	ir er ear (as in earth)	ou oy	ere eer are ear (as in pear)	c k ck ch	ce ci cy sc stl se	ge gi gy dge	le mb kn gn wr	tch sh (as in action) ea (as in head) (w)a
	aw au al	ir er ear (as in earth)	ou oy	ere eer are ear (as in pear)	c k ck ch	ce ci cy sc stl se	ge gi gy dge	le mb kn gn wr	tch sh (as in action) ea (as in head) (w)a
	aw au al	ir er ear (as in earth)	ou oy	ere eer are ear (as in pear)	c k ck ch	ce ci cy sc stl se	ge gi gy dge	le mb kn gn wr	tch sh (as in action) ea (as in head) (w)a
	aw au al	ir er ear (as in earth)	ou oy	ere eer are ear (as in pear)	c k ck ch	ce ci cy sc stl se	ge gi gy dge	le mb kn gn wr	tch sh (as in action) ea (as in head) (w)a
	aw au al	ir er ear (as in earth)	ou oy	ere eer are ear (as in pear)	c k ck ch	ce ci cy sc stl se	ge gi gy dge	le mb kn gn wr	tch sh (as in action) ea (as in head) (w)a

Appendix 9: Word lists from *Letters and Sounds*, Phases 2 to 5

Phase 2

Letters	Set 1				Set 2				Set 3			
	s	a	t	p	i	n	m	d	g	o	c	k
Example words for reading and spelling				at	it	an	am	and	tag	got	can	kid
				sat	is	in	man	Dad	gag	on	cot	kit
				pat	sit	nip	mam	sad	gig	not	cop	Kim
				tap	sat	pan	mat	dim	gap	pot	cap	Ken
				sap	pit	pin	map	dip	nag	top	cat	
					tip	tin	Pam	din	sag	dog	cod	
					pip	tan	Tim	did	gas	pop		
					sip	nap	Sam	Sid	pig	God		
									dig	Mog		
High frequency words (*in italics*) and tricky words (in bold)								*and*		*got*	*can*	*to*
										on		
										not		

Phase 2

	Set 4				Set 5				
Letters	ck	e	u	r	h	b	f ff	l ll	ss
Example words	kick, sock sack, dock pick, sick pack, ticket pocket	get, pet, ten net, pen, peg met, men neck	up, mum run, mug cup, sun tuck, mud sunset	rim, rip, ram rat, rag, rug rot, rocket carrot	had, him, his hot, hut, hop hum, hit, hat has, hack, hug	but, big, back bet, bad, bag bed, bud beg, bug, bun bus, Ben, bat bit, bucket beckon, rabbit	of, if, off, fit fin, fun, fig fog, puff, huff cuff, fan, fat	lap, let, leg lot, lit, bell fill, doll, tell sell, Bill, Nell dull, laptop	ass less, hiss mass, mess boss, fuss hiss, pass, kiss Tess, fusspot
High frequency words (in *italics*) and tricky words (in bold)		*get*	*up, mum* **the, no, go**	*rim*	*had*	*but*	*of, if, off*		**I, into**

* In the North of England the letter a is pronounced /a/.

Phase 3

	Set 6				Set 7			New graphemes							
Letters	j	v	w	x	y	Z zz	qu	ch	sh	th	ng	ai	ee	igh	oa
Example words	jam Jill jet jog Jack Jen jet-lag jacket	van vat vet Vic Ravi Kevin visit velvet	will win wag web wig wax cobweb wicked	mix, fix box, tax six, taxi vixen exit	yap yes yet yell yum- yum	zip Zak buzz jazz zigzag	quiz quit quick quack liquid	chop chin chug check such chip chill much rich chicken	ship shop shed shell fish shock cash bash hush rush	them then that, this with moth thin thick path* bath*	ring rang hang song wing rung king long sing ping-pong	wait Gail hail pain aim sail main tail rain bait	see feel weep feet jeep seem meet week deep keep	high sigh light might night right sight fight tight tonight	coat load goat loaf road soap oak toad foal boatman
High frequency words (in italics) and tricky (in bold)				me be			*he* *my* *by*			*them* *then* *that* *this* *with*	**they** **she**				

* In the North of England the letter a is pronounced /a/.

New graphemes

Letters	long oo	short oo	ar	or	ur	ow	oi	ear	air	ure	er
Example words	too, zoo boot, hoof zoom, cool food, root moon rooftop	look, foot cook good book took wood wool, hook hood	bar, car bark, card cart, hard jar, park market farmyard	for, fork cord, cork sort, born worn, fort torn cornet	fur, burn urn, burp curl, hurt surf, turn turnip curds	now down owl cow how bow pow! row town towel	oil, boil coin, coil join, soil toil, quoit poison tinfoil	ear dear fear hear gear near tear year rear beard	air, fair hair, lair pair, cairn	sure lure assure insure pure cure secure manure mature	hammer letter rocker ladder supper dinner boxer better summer banner
High frequency words (in italics) and tricky words (in bold)	*too*	*look* **we** **are**		*for*		*now* *down*	**you** **her**				**all** **was**

	Phase 4						
	CVCC words						
	Words using sets 1–7 letters			**Words using Phase 3 graphemes**		**Polysyllabic words**	
Example words	*went*	best	fond	champ	shift	*children*	shampoo
	it's	tilt	gust	chest	shelf	helpdesk	Chester
	help	lift	hand	tenth	joint	sandpit	giftbox
	just	lost	next	theft	boost	windmill	shelter
	tent	tuft	milk	Welsh	thump	softest	lunchbox
	belt	damp	golf	chimp	paint	pondweed	sandwich
	hump	bust	jump	bench	roast	desktop	shelving
	band	camp	fact	sixth	toast	helper	Manchester
	dent	gift	melt	punch	beast	handstand	chimpanzee
	felt	kept		chunk	think	melting	champion
	gulp	tusk		thank	burnt	seventh	thundering
	lamp	limp	ask*				
	wind	soft	fast*				
	hump	pond	last*				
	land	husk	daft*				
	nest	cost	task*				
	link	bunk					
	hunt						
High frequency words (*in italics*) and tricky words (in bold)	*went* *it's* *help* *just*					*children*	**said, have, like, so, do some, come were, there little, one when, out what**

* In the North of England the letter a is pronounced /a/.

Phase 4					
CCV and CCVC words					
	Words using sets 1–7 letters		**Words using Phase 3 phonemes**		
Example words	*from*	grip	green	flair	clear	speech
	stop	glad	fresh	trail	train	smear
	spot	twin	steep	cream	swing	thrill
	frog	sniff	tree	clown	droop	
	step	plum	spear	star	spoon	
	plan	gran	smell	creep	float	**Polysyllabic words**
	speck	swim	spoil	brown	smart	treetop
	trip	clap	train	stair	groan	starlight
	grab	drop	spoon	spoil	brush	floating
	track		sport	spark	growl	freshness
	spin	glass*	thrush	bring	scoop	
	flag	grass*	trash	crash	sport	
		brass*	start	bleed	frown	
High frequency words (in italics)	*from*					

* In the North of England the letter a is pronounced /a/.

Phase 4					
CVCC, CCCVC and CCCVCC words					
	Words using sets 1–7 letters			**Words using Phase 3 graphemes**	**Polysyllabic words**
Example words	stand	crust		crunch	driftwood
	crisp	tramp	graft*	drench	twisting
	trend	grunt	grant*	trench	printer
	trust	crept	blast*	Grinch	
	spend	drift	grasp*	shrink	
	glint	slept	slant*	thrust	
	twist	skunk			
	brand	think		spring	
	frost	thank		strap	
	cramp	blink		string	
	plump	drank		scrap	
	stamp	blank		street	
	blend	trunk		scrunch	
	stunt				

* In the North of England the letter a is pronounced /a/.

Phase 5								
New graphemes for reading								
ay	**ou**	**ie**	**ea**	**oy**	**ir**	**ue**	**ue**	
day	*out*	pie	sea	boy	girl	clue	cue	
play	*about*	lie	seat	toy	sir	blue	due	
may	cloud	tie	bead	joy	bird	glue	hue	
say	scout	die	read	oyster	shirt	true	venue	
stray	found	cried	meat	Roy	skirt	Sue	value	
clay	proud	tried	treat	destroy	birth	Prue	pursue	
spray	sprout	spied	heap	Floyd	third	rue	queue	
tray	sound	fried	least	enjoy	first	flue	statue	
crayon	loudest	replied	steamy	royal	thirteen	issue	rescue	
delay	mountain	denied	repeat	annoying	thirsty	tissue	argue	
aw	**wh**		**ph**	**ew**		**oe**	**au**	**ey**
saw	*when*	who	Philip	blew	stew	toe	Paul	money
paw	*what*	whose	Philippa	chew	few	hoe	haul	honey
raw	which	whole	phonics	grew	new	doe	daub	donkey
claw	where	whom	sphinx	drew	dew	foe	launch	cockney
jaw	why	whoever	Christopher	screw	pew	woe	haunted	jockey
lawn	whistle		dolphin	crew	knew	Joe	Saul	turkey
yawn	whenever		prophet	brew	mildew	goes	August	chimney
law	wheel		phantom	flew	nephew	tomatoes	jaunty	valley
shawl	whisper		elephant	threw	renew	potatoes	author	trolley
drawer	white		alphabet	Andrew	Matthew	heroes	automatic	monkey
a-e	**e-e**	**i-e**	**o-e**	**u-e**				
came	these	*like*	bone	June	huge			
made	Pete	*time*	pole	flute	cube			
make	Eve	pine	home	prune	tube			
take	Steve	ripe	alone	rude	use			
game	even	shine	those	rule	computer			
race	theme	slide	stone					
same	gene	prize	woke					
snake	scene	nice	note					
amaze	complete	invite	explode					
escape	extreme	inside	envelope					
High frequency words in italics								

Phase 5								
Alternative pronunciations of known graphemes for reading								
a				**e**		**i**		
hat	acorn bacon apron angel apricot bagel station nation Amy lady	fast** path** pass** father** bath** last** grass** after** branch** afternoon**	*was* *what* wash wasp squad squash want watch wallet wander	bed	*he* *me* *she* *we* *be* *the** recent frequent region decent	tin	mind find wild pint blind child kind grind behind remind	
o		**u**				**ow**		
hot	*no* *so* *go* *old* *don't* gold cold told both hold	*but*	unit union unicorn music tuba future human stupid duty humour	*put*** pull** push** full** bush** bull** cushion** awful** playful** pudding**	down	low grow snow glow bowl tow show low window rowing- boat		
* Before a vowel ** South of England only								
High frequency words in italics								

Phase 5									
ie		**ea**		**er**		**ou**			
pie	chief brief field shield priest yield shriek thief relief belief	sea	head dead deaf ready bread heaven feather pleasant instead breakfast	farmer	*her* fern stern Gerda herbs jerky perky Bernard servant permanent	out	*you* soup group	*could* would should	mould shoulder boulder
y				**ch**			**c**		
yes	*by* *my* try why dry fry sky spy fry reply	gym crystal mystery crystal pyramid Egypt bicycle Lynne cygnet rhythm	*very* happy funny carry hairy smelly penny crunchy lolly merrily	chin	school Christmas chemist chord chorus Chris chronic chemical headache technical	chef Charlene Chandry Charlotte machine brochure chalet	cat	cell central acid cycle icy cent Cynthia success December accent	
g		**ey**							
got	gent gym gem Gill gentle ginger Egypt magic danger energy	money	*they* grey obey prey survey						

Phase 5							
Alternative spellings for each phoneme							
/ch/		**/j/**	**/m/**	**/n/**		**/r/**	
picture	catch	fudge	lamb	gnat	knit	wrap	
adventure	fetch	hedge	limb	gnaw	knob	wren	
creature	pitch	bridge	comb	gnash	knot	wrong	
future	notch	ledge	climb	gnome	knee	wrench	
nature	crutch	nudge	crumb	sign	knock	write	
capture	stitch	badge	dumb	design	knife	wrote	
feature	match	lodge	thumb	resign	know	wreck	
puncture	ditch	podgy	numb		knew	wry	
signature	kitchen	badger	plumbing		knight	written	
mixture	scratchy	dodging	bomber		knuckle	wretched	
/s/		**/z/**	**/u/***	**/i/**		**/ear/**	
listen	house	please	*some*	happy	donkey	*here*	beer
whistle	mouse	tease	*come*	sunny	valley	mere	deer
bristle	grease	ease	done	mummy	monkey	severe	jeer
glisten	cease	rouse	none	daddy	chimney	interfere	cheer
Christmas	crease	browse	son	only	trolley	Windermere	peer
rustle	horse	cheese	nothing	gym	pulley	adhere	sneer
jostle	gorse	noise	month	crystal	Lesley		sheer
bustle	purse	pause	mother	mystery			veer
castle	grouse	blouse	worry	sympathy			career
wrestling	loose	because	brother	pyramid			steering
*The phoneme /u/ is not generally used in North of England accents							
High frequency words in italics							

Phase 5							
/ar/		**/air/**			**/or/**		
father	half	*there*	pear	bare	all	four	caught
lather	calf	*where*	bear	care	always	pour	taught
rather	almond	nowhere	wear	dare	talk	your	naughty
pass*	calm	somewhere	tear	fare	walk	court	haughty
path*	qualm	everywhere	swear	hare	wall	fourth	daughter
bath*	lip balm			mare	fall	Seymour	Vaughan
last*	palm tree			square	ball	tour*	
grass*				scare	hall	mourn*	
afternoon*				stare	calling	fourteen	
branching*				share	beanstalk	tournament	
*The classification of these words is very dependent on accent							
/ur/		**/oo/**		**/ai/**			
learn	word	*could*	*put*	*day*	*came*		
earn	work	*would*	pull	*play*	*made*		
earth	world	*should*	push	*may*	*make*		
pearl	worm		full	say	take		
early	worth		bush	stray	game		
search	worse		bull	clay	race		
heard	worship		cushion	spray	same		
earnest	worthy		pudding	tray	snake		
rehearsal	worst		playful	crayon	amaze		
				delay	escape		

Phase 5									
/ee/					**/igh/**				
sea	these	happy	chief	key	pie	*by*	*like*	
seat	Pete	sunny	brief	donkey	lie	*my*	*time*	
bead	Eve	mummy	field	valley	tie	try	pine	
read	Steve	daddy	shield	monkey	cried	why	ripe	
meat	even	only	priest	chimney	tried	dry	shine	
treat	theme	funny	yield	trolley	spied	fry	slide	
heap	complete	sadly	shriek	pulley	fried	sky	prize	
least	Marlene	penny	thief	Lesley	replied	spy	nice	
steamy	gene	heavy	relief	money	applied	deny	decide	
repeat	extreme	quickly	belief	honey	denied	reply	polite	
/oa/			**/(y) oo/**				**/oo/**		
low	toe	bone	cue	tune	stew	clue	June	blew
grow	hoe	pole	due	cube	few	blue	flute	chew
snow	doe	home	hue	tube	new	glue	prune	grew
glow	foe	woke	venue	use	dew	true	rude	drew
bowl	woe	those	value	cute	pew	Sue	fluke	screw
tow	Joe	stone	pursue	duke	knew	Prue	brute	crew
show	goes	woke	queue	huge	mildew	rue	spruce	brew
slow	Glencoe	note	statue	mule	nephew	flue	plume	flew
window	heroes	phone	rescue	amuse	renew	issue	rule	threw
rowing	echoes	alone	argue	computer	Matthew	tissue	conclude	Andrew
boat								

Phase 5			
/sh/			
special	station	sure	chef
official	patience	sugar	Charlotte
social	caption	passion	Charlene
artificial	mention	session	Michelle
facial	position	mission	Chandry

Phase 5
New phoneme
treasure
television
vision
pleasure
leisure
beige
visual
measure
usual
casual

INDEX INDEX INDEX INDEX INDEX INDEX INDEX